LAW
UNIVERSAL

AF471717

FRANCIS YAO **DJABAKU**

AuthorHouse™
1663 Liberty Drive
Bloomington, IN 47403
www.authorhouse.com
Phone: 1-800-839-8640

Published by AuthorHouse 03/21/2013

ISBN: 978-1-4772-7117-9 (sc)
ISBN: 978-1-4772-7118-6 (hc)
ISBN: 978-1-4772-7116-2 (e)

Library of Congress Control Number: 2012917456

CONTENTS

ACKNOWLEDGEMENTS

I am grateful to all who sacrificed their secret thoughts and writings and impacted the Universal Law into the life of the Author; for their vision and support in writing this book. I am especially grateful to their intelligence, and their interest in this book. Since all these people whose name is not mentioned in this work have contributed diverse ways in bringing this book to a successful completion, I absolve all of them from any short coming of this work; all shortcomings are entirely my responsibility.

PREFACE

To learn from this Book is to enter a world that is strange to the modern mind, but, not to the already initiated. This is a work that explains the thought of the ancient Near East; the Modern Wests' scientific, religious and philosophical way of thinking.

Thinking into the minds of men like Moses, David, Solomon, Shedriach, Meshach and Abednego. Greatest like Jesus, Mohammed, Krishna; now men like Haile Sellasei of Ethiopia, the legendary priest of Ashanti Empire—Okomfo Anokye and host of others.

Revealing the teachings of His Majesty; destroying the teachings of the devils philosophy.

Unvailing the application of Mathematics in persons life.

INTRODUCTION

After reading and learning from this book, you will be able, to find in this world—Salvation—Self realization. You will be able to think correctly, and act courageously. You will discover that, there is no effect, without a cause. In a plain man's language; nothing happens, without a cause.

You will get the knowledge, that, there is one Universal Law, for every single living thing in the world, or in the universe. A Law that is inevitable or unchangeable; the fact and the truth. A Universal Law that is well accepted, by great minds in philosophy, science and religion.

This book, will try to blow your mind, get you confused but will be firm, decisive, and not confused. This book, will make you understand what? Universal Law, will energize you, bring out the best out of the best in you. Yes, the very best, in you.

It will kill fear, in you. Re-create all the courageous conquering principles, of practical and applied psychology, in you.

With the understanding of Constructive Thought, you will lead and not follow. You will win, and not lose. In place of failure, success. This book will return you back to Culture, the Bible, the Quran; the Holy Shiva Purana. Depending on the mindset of your religion. Making you observant of your environment. Destroying the bad, and improving on the good. Combing positive and negative, for a rightful purpose. Applying God, and rejecting the devil.

This book is making science, religion and philosophy one. This book is confirming cause and effect, one air, one earth, one sun, and one Universal Law.

This book will tell of you, me and all—the beginning, the middle and the end. Yes! this book is Constructive.

How to learn form this book

Read it slowly; number by number; frequently and silently. Understand each sentence in a number. Meditate on it frequently.

CHAPTER 1

DISCOVER HOW TO THINK CORRECTLY AND ACT COURAGEOUSLY

Moses, founder of Judaism; Jesus, founder of Christianity; Muhammad of Islam, Euclid, the man who made Mathematics famous; Archimedes, the famous scientist, and Socrates, the famous philosopher are vivid illustrations of Constructive Thought. By their teachings one must be born again, repent, renew-his-mind, regeneration, self-realization, salvation, ere he can see the kingdom of heaven and so on. This book is confirming their words which are the Word; and the word teaches what is truth and good and truth and good teach what is false and evil. Unless man knows these he cannot possibly be regenerated, for he remains in his evils and their falsities, calling the former good and the latter truth. The fundamental principle for regeneration is temptation, natural or spiritual. The Universal Law makes people learn through suffering and uses distress to open their eyes and this is the modus operandi of the teachings of the Universal Law through temptations. Planning and thought lies at the bottom of everything that is done. The mind concerns itself primarily with four things: these are good and evil and life and death. They all begin in the mind but the tongue is their absolute ruler and their basic or fundamental rule reveals causes and effect.

1. The laws under which we live are designed solely for our benefit or advantage. These laws are immutable and we cannot escape from their operation. All the great eternal forces act in solemn silence, but it is in our power to place ourselves in harmony with them and therefore express a life of comparative peace, and happiness. Difficulties, distress, obstacles, indicate that we are either refusing to give out what we no longer need or refusing to accept what we require for further growth.

2. Growth is attained through an exchange of the old for the new; of the good for the better. It is a conditional or reciprocal thought entity, and the completeness makes it possible for us to receive only as we give.
   (Cast your bread upon the waters and after many days you will find it is a fact, faith, and the truth.)

3. We cannot obtain what we lack if we tenaciously cling to what we have. All conditions and experiences that come to us do for our benefit. Difficulties and obstacles will continue to come until we absorb their wisdom and gather from them

the essentials of further growth. That we reap what we sow is mathematical exact.

4. Some men and women seem to attract success, power, wealth, attainment, with very little conscious effort; others conquer with great difficulties; still others fail altogether to reach their ambitions, desires or ideas. Why is this so? Why should some men realize their ambitions easily, others with difficulty and still others not at all; the cause cannot be physical, else the most perfect men, physically, would be the most successful. The difference therefore must be mental, must be in the mind; hence the mind being the creative force must constitute the sole difference between men. It is the mind therefore which overcomes environment and every other obstacle in the path of men and women. The mind connects; links the spirit and the physical together. Hence the mind is the meeting point for the soul and body.

   (Let me recall . . . a friend once sent me a message, and in it was written: "Do not chase after the world and lose your soul". I meditated upon it for quite some time, and had a conclusion; that I should not follow after the crowd or simply put, the masses, and lose my aim (soul). I agree with him because the masses never rule and has never ruled before, they follow.)

5. It is the actualization of interior qualities through the creative power of thought which has given us great leaders like Alexander the great, Napoleon Bonaparte of France,

Dr. J. B. Danquah, and George Washington. Captains of industry like John D. Rockefeller, Bill Gates, Micheal Dell, and Alhaji Asumal Banda. Great inventors like George Stephenson, Archimedes of Greece, Isaac Newton, and Apostle Kwadwo Safo Kantanka. Entertainers like Reggie Rockstone, Mohammed Ali, Mr. Michael Jackson, Michael Jordan, Bob N. Marley, Pele of Brazil, Diego Maradona, Arnold Schwarzenegger and host of others.

6. But such results cannot be secured without proper application, diligence, and concentration.
   (Concentration is very vital in human affairs, considering a footballer on the pitch of football. First they control their intellect and focus all their mind, spirit, eyes on the one football that is being played. It could be a tennis ball, basket ball, a rapper on stage and so on. The well focused once are the ones who attain fame, and then are honored. Every sports person, entertainer etc. wants to be honored, so they develop seriously their concentration level to be the best ever that they can.)

7. The eye is the greediest thing on earth, that is why it is the eye that cries when it's desires are not available or are not met. As you constructively plan in life, in your thoughts you should have an eye to succeed, in whatever you do. These qualities must be part of you—vision, punctuality, attitude, humility, honesty, gentleness, patient, and being sincere.

8. The actualization of interior quality does not come on a silver platter. You have to work for it. Your first plan is that, you should have a vision—what you want to do. You certainly need to acquire a good profession and not a bad one.

9. You need to be very punctual in whatever you do. It is the soul of success. At work, School or whatever thing that you do, cultivate the habit of puntuality. Cease going school or work late. If you practice it often, it will become part of you. See, whilst you are punctual, you have time to plan and do the right thing. But if you are cultured to lateness you do things in perplex, making a lot of mistakes.

10. Watch very carefully your attitude—it will speak a lot about you, accept change. Do not ever make such comments as "that is how I am. I cannot change, I am not in school, worship, business to please anybody".

11. Admit your short coming and learn from them. Do not defend your mistakes. Learn to overcome problems as you grow up. Do not run away from them since you will meet them in your life again. Face all problems squarely as a boxer in a ring of boxing, and conquer them. This is a sure signpost to success.

12. Be honest to yourself and to your neighbor. For it is one of the best principles in life. Do not lie to your neighbour. It would do you no good. Being honest will take you up to so many winning post than lies.

13. Observe to understand that, gentleness, patient, and being sincere to your environment will be to your advantage. Do not rush to react to attacks. In your class of business, religious group, it can happen that your mates, friends, your brothers or sisters at home may act badly against you, take time to re-act. You will be the odd one if you re-act without patience and gentleness to pay back for wrong doing.

14. Spend good time to know your God. Read the Bible, the Koran, and the Holy Shiva Purana, that is if you are a Christian, a Muslim, and a Hindu respectively; make every effort to live by the words in the good books. You could be a traditionalist. You are all in the soup of religion. Yours is to know your God. If you are able to achieve this, greed, envy, and stubbornness will surely die from your life. You will become a success and not a failure, if you read it frequently—the Bible or the Koran or the Shiva Purana.

15. Plan whatever you do from your learning of wisdom. Even in your learning plan your life when it comes to education, religion, family, and business; and what you will do in future. Laziness will not take you anywhere.

16. A successful businessman or student, learns, study, or train while others are sleeping; work while others are loafing; prepares while others are playing and dream to vision himself while others are idling.

17 Business organizations or a student who learns that power comes from within that he is weak only because he has depended on help from outside and who unhesitantly throws himself on his own thought, instantly rights himself, stands erect, assumes a dominant attitude, and works miracles.

18. Be selective in making friends; do not call anybody your friend. Pick friends who will make you sit up, advice, support, plan with you, and most importantly, who has a vision. Remember always that your destiny is in your own hands. And the best way to predict the future is to create it yourself.

19. The reason we have not manifested more faith is because of our lack of understanding of the things in the mental world. We have not understood that everything works in exact accordance with definite laws. Because everything that an individual does on this earth, there is a law for it or in place of it as there is in mathematics, physics, chemistry, natural laws, and so on.
(When the power of thought is fully understood, thought undivided or undivided attention, sincere thought, thinking-thinking, I mean! You will not be thinking of one thing and another at the same time! "Proverbs 4:20-23". It should not be a normal thing to see for example, a student learning and at the same time listening to music or watching television, it's effect will be seen to be marvelous because the cause is constructively done. It is a serious minded endeavor, intense with a singleness of purpose, such that you cannot

be distracted by anything that is not related to your goal. In-fact, you use your intellect to shut out all destructions and refuse to let your mind wander around and then, concentrate passionately on your purpose).

20. The law of thought is as definite as the law of mathematics or the law of gravity or the law of chemistry or the law of electricity. When we begin to understand that happiness, health, success, prosperity and every other condition or environment are results, and that these results are created by right thinking, either consciously or unconsciously. To be in ignorance of the laws governing in the mental world is to be like child playing with fire or a man manipulating powerful chemicals without a knowledge of their nature, or relations.

21. This is universally true, because the mind is the one great cause which produces all conditions in the lives of men and women. Man is continually reaping the fruits of his own words. A little reflection will convince us that all the great laws of "NATURE" operates in silence and that, the underlying principle is the Law of Attraction.
    (It is as magnetic forces attracting each other, when you consistently say positive words into the air, that is what you surely will see happening in your life, said either consciously or unconsciously. Your life circumstances today has been what you thought of yesterday and your tomorrow will be what you are thinking of to-day. Now, let us say that you are most often saying "I cannot be sick in my life, and that I will always live above sickness and be healthy". You surely

attract health to yourself, either you said it knowingly or unknowingly. It is as if, the Gods are really blessing you but that is the truth. Well accepted fact married to the truth. Theologians, philosophers and religious leaders accepts this fact which has been known far back two thousand years ago, even before the birth of Jesus of Nazareth, Mohammed the founder of Islamic religion, and so on. The formula cannot be changed, for it is clear to all great thinkers).

22. There is power in words followed by action even more, followed by conviction. He who discovers this becomes a genius to his generations even to the far yet unborn.

23. Silence is power, for in silence we can think. It is only destructive processes such as earth-quakes, tornadoes and catastrophes that employ forces. Nothing good is ever accomplished in that way. True courage is cool, calm, and collected and is never foolhardy, quarrelsome, ill-natured or contentious.
    (Let us think about the great teacher named Jesus Christ of Nazareth, when he was captured with force, he was never foolhardy quarrelsome, and so on. But the opposition used the vice versa and ended up losers. The same applies to Nelson Mandela of South Africa and a host of others).

24. Accumulation in the arsenal to reserve and preserve a part of the supply which we are constantly receiving, so as to be in position to take advantage of the larger opportunities which will come as soon as we are ready for them. Has it not

been said, "To him that hath shall be given" All successful business men have this qualities well developed.
(Just consider an up-coming, and a talented musician; he pens down his Inspirations "lyrics" so that one day he can record a full album of many tracks. Then comes in a producer or record label)

25. One of the modus operands of the Universal Law is that; it uses what you have to bless you. Those seemingly little things you have is what it uses to produce a miracle for you. Read in the bible 2 Kings 4:1-7.

26. I read about James Hills and host of others, who died not long ago, but probably before I was born in the 1960s leaving an estate of probably $12,000,000 said, if you want to know whether you are destiny to be a success or a failure in life, you can easily find out. The test is simple, cheap, and it is infallible; are you able to save money? If not, drop out. You will lose. You may think not but you will lose as sure as you live. The seed of success is not in you. The fruit of this knowledge is as it were, a gift of the Gods; it is the truth that makes men free, not only free from lack and limitation, but free from sorrow, worry and care and is it not wonderful to realize that this law is no respecter of persons, that it makes no difference what your habits of thought maybe, the way has been prepared. Proverbs 23:19.

27. Silence thought, is after all, the mightiest agent in human affairs, in-fact, a pure brokalist. The happiness of your life

depends upon the quality of your thoughts. Therefore, guard accordingly, and take care that you entertain no notions unsuitable to virtue and reasonable nature.

28. Man is his own enemy. And of his own enemy is called fear. Fear is the devil itself, known for it's stealing, famously—its fundamental principle is to steal. It is the worst of all the results of human being's wrong thinking, it is at the bottom of it all. The father of all negative thoughts.

29. Thought engenders thought. Place one idea upon paper, another will follow and still another until you have written a page. You cannot fathom your mind. It is a well of thought which has no bottom. The more you draw from it, the clearer and fruitful it will be.
(Thinking of your church pastor, your imam or your priest, it would be observed that the more they read through the Bible, the Koran, the Hindu verdict or literature or the Holy Shiva Purana and meditates upon it the more their understanding will be on it. The same applies to your school teacher, even you! The church member, the Muslim, Hindu, traditionalist, students, and so on.)

30. If you neglect to think yourself, and use other people's thoughts, giving them utterances only, you will never know what you are capable of.

31. Learning without thought is labour lost; thought without learning is perilous. Thinkers are as scarce gold, but he

whose thoughts embrace all their subject, who pursues it uninterruptedly, and fearless of consequences, is a diamond of enormous size.

32. A little reflection will confirm the saying that:" The earth itself will give you an answer if you humbly ask it whether it produce more gold, silver, copper, iron, lead or clay. There is more silver than gold, more copper than silver, more iron than copper, more lead than iron and more clay than lead". Which are more desirable and valuable? He who has what is scarce has more reason to be pleased than the person who has what is plentiful. Of all the six, where do you belong?

33. The Universal Law is fundamental to every thing that is seen or created. Anyone who does not know this is simply foolish. Such individuals look at the good things around them and still fail to see the law that brought them about. They have studied the things made out of it but they have not recognized the laws that brought them about.
(This is like admiring Christians and not knowing Jesus Christ or Muslims and knowing nothing about Mohammed. Even more knowing a lot about cars and not knowing their inventors or manufacturers.)

34. Instead, they suppose that the gods who rule the world are fire or wind or stone or the circling stars or rushing water or heavenly bodies.

35. Truly people were so delighted with the beauty of these things that they thought they must be gods, but they fail to realize that these things have a source, and that the source is master of them all, for out of it came their beauty. They lack the wisdom, knowledge and an understanding of the word causes, but are well knowledgeable on effects

36. Since people are amazed at the power of these things, and how they behave, they ought to learn or study in silence from them that their source is far more powerful. If we are able to see or realize how vast and beautiful creation is then we are learning about the Universal Law at the same time either consciously or unconsciously.

37. But, maybe, you and I are too harsh with these people. After all, they may have really wanted to find the Universal Law usually called God in religion, but they could not. Surrounded by the works of the Universal Law, they keep on looking at them, until they are finally convinced that because the things they see are so beautiful and more than much of their understanding, they must be gods.

38. But still, these individuals really have no excuse. If they had enough intelligence to speculate about the nature of the universe, why did they never find the laws governing them? One thing is for sure; knowing the laws is gaining righteousness and applying them as your right or power is where immortality begins

39. Ninety-five percent of the people are busily or busy attempting to change effects with effects. Something happens which they do not like and they try to change the situation. They soon find that they are simply changing one form of distress for another. The other five percent are busily engage with causes. They know that in other to make any permanent change, it is the cause which they must seek. They soon find that the cause is within their control. It is five percent who do the thinking and the ninety-five percent who merely accept the thought of others. It is those only who think who can feel a thing before it happens.

40. We know constructively that all truly wise thoughts have been thought already long ago, thousands of times and millions of years; but to make them truly ours, we must think them over again honestly, till they take root in our personal experiences. For instance, when there are weeds in your environment and you want to get rid of it, you do not weed it with cutlass but with hoe, uprooting the roots of the weeds from the soil.
(Moses was a great thinker—that is, he could think to the point of even thinking one-on-one with the Universal Power or Spirit, in total, the Universal Law usually called God in religion. I cannot forget off Muhammad, the founder of Islam. Think of his impacts on this generation. Krishna of the Hindu fame, with him we are able to discover this great arcana—omnipotent, omnipresent, omniscient, which are derived from the ancient word Omkara, and in short Om. To this generation in Christendom, it is known as the Holy Bible or Jesus Christ or Jesus for short in English. But English is a

young language because we know that the original English people spoke Celtic. But the word Om is still in existence among the Hindus—in Hinduism. This tells us that, English is a constructive language; every word has its cause or source. The son of man, Jesus of Nazareth considered to be the greatest worker of miracles, and so on, was the greater thinker probably. He used to separate himself from the masses to a quite place on the mountain to think alone. Luke 5;16.

41. The idea that there is a phenomenon called Black Magic is attributed to credulity, superstition, and a lack of understanding of the laws governing mental world.

42. We are human beings, so-called. We had a beginning not so many years ago. There was a point of conception when the physical body began to take form, and gradually it developed and grew in the womb of the mother until the time came to be born. We were all born, we all went through this cycle, and here we are to prove it. Obviously there was something that made this miracle possible. It did not just happen by chance. There was very definite principle involved in the process. But this form which came forth, compose of physical substance, also developed some other capacities beside the physical.

43. The mind, the capacity of mind, developed and grew, and capacity to experience emotion. They were not ready—made, were they? They developed and grew to the extent that we know them at this point. So we could recognize easily

enough that these are also part of the physical form. See, the external form includes the physical form and the emotional form, if we could put it that way. That is more or less what most people know of themselves, a capacity or capacities capable of being used for some purpose here on earth. What purpose? Few people seem to know, although they devise purposes of various sorts or kinds.

45. This external form is nothing off itself. It is what is described as the soul, in the bible. The soul of human being has beginning at the point conception, and it has an ending somewhere along the line. There are two possibilities with respect to the ending, but at the moment the experience of the form seems to be inevitable without any alternative.

46. When we are born into the world we are born seemingly under sentence of the law of death: an interesting fact which is discouraging to many people, and it does not seem as though we could easily believe in a Universal Law of love if we accept this idea as being the way it seems.

47. Everyone on the face of the earth is born into the world, and immediately we are on death row, under the law or sentence of death. Sometimes we can manage to get a reprieve for a while, but the execution finally is seemingly inevitable.

48. One thing is for sure—there is no mountain (discouragement) anywhere, but our lack of understanding of the Universal Law has made it so! This is a great arcana and need to be unfold.

It has to do with our thinking and faith in the Universal Energy—Science; the Universal principle—philosophy; and the Universal Spirit—religion. In all, there is one omnipotent, omniscient, omnipresent power therefore one Universal Law in religion usually called GOD. This is because we have been told and have been learning and have understood by earlier reformers we have good and bad in philosophy; positive and negative in science and god and the devil in religion. This is not just a mere theory for confirmation of what I am saying or statement, but a pure fact married to the truth. Everything being talked about concerning thought in this book is base on this three facts—philosophy, science, and religion, and their foundations are causes and effects.

49. If you are zealous to understanding the word causes, you will be able to change problems to challenges. If you are positive-minded, you would like to face every challenge. Negative-minded people see challenges as problem. Zeal is contagious. It motivates people and inspires others also. So spread zeal in your team starting from yourself for man does not take away from himself but himself.

50. Zeal builds confidence inside. It is a window of your mind from where you can throw all your worries, tensions, and upsetting matters. Self-realization is necessary to live self, and zeal helps you realize your strengths and weakness. Once you identify your weaknesses, it helps you to overcome them. Enthusiasm is fuel for self-motivation. Just call yourself and be zealous in your purpose.

51. Thoughts of all kinds are held in solution in the Universal Mind or Will. Because mind is will. Please remember that when you say something like: this is the Mind of God, it is the same as this is the Will of God.

(We are each individual mind in the universal mind or will. For instance, we have a universal name called Jesus or James but there are so many individuals by name Jesus or James. So when we are calling the name out of the universal, we have to be specific like Jesus Christ or Jesus of Nazareth, then we can know who exactly we are calling out of the universal name. This is the truth accepted in science, philosophy, and theology or religion. Let us use for an instance here, the bible or the book of Isaiah to be specific; we have two different Isaiah's in there who did the performances. There is one called Isaiah of Jerusalem who wrote the chapter (1) one to chapter (39) thirty-nine and Isaiah of exile who wrote the chapter (40) forty to chapter 66) sixty-six. This is a fact by theologians. Let us not forget that they went into real thinking. They thought of it, calculated it constructively. Again, let us use a 'picture' of a particular person by name Josephine. We know that the name Josephine is for females and there are so many female by that name Josephine in the world. This makes the name Josephine a universal name. I might go to some group of people having their own discussion and ask for help that: "Excuse me guys, I am looking for Josephine". It will sound insane to them because there may be six, seven people named Josephine in that particular community. But if I have the picture of the one particular Josephine I am looking for it will not take me much stress to locate Josephine. As it is in the physical, so it is in the spiritual or the mental world. This is what has made the image worship a vital part of the Christendom especially when dealing with the saints specifically the Roman Catholic or the Hindus Worshipers)

52. The individual may open his mental gates and thereby become receptive to thoughts of any kind or description. If he thinks that there are magicians, witches or wizards who are desirous of injuring him. He is thereby opening the door for the entrance of such thoughts and he will be able to say with Job "The things that I feared have come upon me". If on the contrary, he thinks that there are those desirous of helping him, he will find that "as thy faith is, so be it unto thee" is as true today as it was two thousand years ago.

53. Self-denial is not success. We cannot give unless we get; we cannot be helpful unless we are strong. The secret of power is service. Wealth must be correctly used. It is not right for someone who is selfish to be rich. What use is money to a stingy person?

54. If you deny yourself in order to accumulate wealth, you are accumulating it for someone else. Others will use your riches to live in luxury. How can you generous with others if are stingy with yourself, if you are not willing to enjoy your own wealth? No one is worse off than someone who is stingy with himself. It is an evil effect that brings is own punishment. When such a person does something good, it

is only by accident; his selfishness will sooner or later be evident. This is nothing but the truth!

55. A selfish person is evil; he turns his back on people's need and is never satisfied with what he has. Greed will shrivel up a person's soul. Some people are too stingy to put bread on their own table and I have witnessed it over and over and so on.

56. We must remember that death is coming for us someday and we have not been told when that will be. But before that day comes, be kind to your friends; be as generous as you can. Do not deny yourself a single day's happiness. If there is anything you want to do and it is lawful, go ahead! Someday all that you have worked for will be divided up, and given to others. The ancient law decrees that we must die.

57. See! Human beings are like leaves on a spreading tree. New growth takes the place of the fallen leaves; while some of us die; others are being born—philosophy.

58. Jesus Christ is gone, and Christian are in place of him now. Mohammad is gone, and Muslims are in place of him now. Christians are living the life and teaching of Jesus Christ, and so are Muslims, the life and teaching of Mohammad which they have heard of from their beginning or from their regeneration. All religions are one, and every religions development depends upon the quality of truth in it. The importance of all religion, science, and philosophy is to

acknowledge the Universal Law consciously, and desist from evil practices.

59. Good religion elevates your thinking and shows you how to improve your conduct or attitude. It supports you in the struggle to do what is right and bring out the best in you.

60. The fundamental fact and truth in every religion is to acknowledge God, and desist from doing evil to the neighbor. For this reason or cause, the Universal Law makes provisions that, this fundamental fact and truth should be in every religion. But the individual should not be trusted. Whether the religion in practice is conscious of Jesus Christ or Mohammed or Krishna consciousness or not, does not prevent a person from gaining happiness in life on earth and after. History guided these people to become what they now stand for! Just know your past and histories and then you will know where you are heading to.
    (There are various kinds of schools both private, and government owned ones, and each one boasting of being the best school is only an advertisement. But at the end they all write the same common final examination as their judgment day of what they have been learning all the while in school. Questions are not discriminated to favor any school. Also, in a kingdom, someone may know the king through the son, someone through his friend, and someone through his servant. Think or meditate on this in Christianity as a good or excellent example——Father, Spirit and Son. Again, a nation or country can have many tribes and still be united as

one. Take Ghana in 'West Africa,' a peaceful country as it is known now, have different kinds of tribes speaking different kinds of languages but so much united living in peace and harmony under one mother called GHANA, formally known as the Gold Coast. Some will understand these sayings, and some will not. Why? Because they say God has made it so. But no! it is because some will think and others will not. It is in our arsenal to think or not to do so. We have control over everything in this world and the mental world. Ours is to place ourselves into the Universal Law. Wisdom is always on our streets, homes, congregations, in-fact everywhere! Our is to see and think it over. Thinking is the hardest work on earth and it makes a man different from a boy. But getting the knowledge and understanding it should not be under-rated. Thinking really makes a man fearful. Think about your cat in your house or a lion in the forest! They are cool, calm, always, observing but anytime they roar against their opponents fear catches them (opponents). They never turn back when they are determined to catch or fight their opponents. In-fact, they are very courageous.)

61. Force is neither created nor destroyed. This is the Om's of the Universal Energy. Force in science makes all things possible. Its pressure is unlimited; the wonderful rules of the Universal Energy which is the under-lying principle, and being the modus-operandi of all work done or inventory.

62. Positive and negative sets into operation forces to act either positively or negatively on any individual or mechanism

that sets itself to operating in it's modus-operandi. This is universally true. This truth has brought about great inventions and acted with its elements either positively or negatively both on the earth and the universe—Bulbs, Motor Cars, Ships, and so on. The force of the mind is so powerful to subjecting every element below it.

63. It is force that holds the world and all that is in it through its attraction law, in-fact, it holds the universe. A scenario is of the law discovered by Isaac Newton——how the (land) earth attracts the fruits of a tree to itself. This is no different in philosophy and religion.
(When you want to do something just be focus on what you are doing. Let nothing distract your purpose.)

64. The explored activities, demonstrated that light passes through some materials like nylon and not through others like a thick blanket. Light rays that does not pass through a material reflect off and reflection means to bounce light rays that are reflected off an opaque surface, they change the direction they are traveling. This is a constructive thought of a natural law.
(When we think positively, we receive positively and likewise negative thoughts such as fear, worries, superstition and self-deprecations brings negative thoughts of the same kind).

65. You see objects because light reflected from the object enters your eyes. A mirror is very smooth, and shiny. When light

rays are reflected from a mirror, they are reflected in the same direction. When you stand in front of a mirror you see a face just like yours. Some people cannot harmonize their view of science with scripture statements, and they think that religion is to be tested by their standard or science false.

66. Let me tell you some histories of one or two inventors. But first, I will write about Dr. Louis Pasteur. Before I begin with his science, do this first.

67. Check your concentration level, and then you can judge yourself to a percentage that you think you deserve. Can you say "Glory to Jesus of Nazareth" for one hundred and eight times without you losing your focus on what you are saying? or "Om Namah Shiva Ya" if you are a Hindu or "Laa Elaaha Illallaah" or " peace and blessing be on the prophet Mohammad" if you are a Muslim respectively—depending on your religious believe. Saying it with your full attention, thought undivided, sincere thought! At this time, you turn off the television, radio, and even the telephone or mobile phone, for there is a matter at hand. You are doing something earnestly to get results. This is a thanksgiving offering. I hope with time you have mastered your concentration level? If yes! Then let us begin with my stories.

68. Because of great men who had thought hard to bring about change, we now live in better homes than our fore-fathers did, and we eat better food than they did. We are more careful about clean clothes and clean bodies than they used to be.

These things have helped to reduce the amount of sickness in the world.

69. In olden times, when doctors knew much less about medicine than they do now, people who were seriously ill very frequently died, even though they were young and strong. The reason is that the doctors who are working in hospitals at the present time understand more about the different kinds of illness and the best ways of curing them than did the doctors of former times.

70. Long ago, the only known cure for any illness was magic. When a man was suffering from any disease, he went to a witch or to a wizard and he was given medicine made up of all sorts of unusual things, even such things as snake skins and the hair of mice. While he was drinking it, he has to pronounce certain words. I am not saying that was bad but what I am saying is that men did not understand illness, and because they did not understand, they were afraid. Their fear led them to put their trust in magic. During the past three or four hundred years, all this has changed.

71. Illness and diseases nearly always bring pain. Our doctors are learning to conquer this, too. There is pain in the world still, but there was much more of it in days gone by. Even as recently as one hundred and fifty years ago, doctors could not help people who were suffering great pain. In particular, the soldiers of the army suffered terribly. If a soldier was wounded in a battle so badly that perhaps, his leg had to be

cut off, the operation was performed while the poor soldier was awake and able to feel everything that was being done to him.

72. Nowadays in such cases, the doctors give the soldier a special medicine which sends him to sleep to that he feels no pain at all while they are performing the operation. The discovery of that medicine called chloroform was made more than one hundred years ago by an English Doctor, Sir James Simpson. His discovery has been so successful that it has been applied to quite small operations.

73. If a person has minutes to pull it out, he makes the patient breathe in chloroform, or another similar medicine, which has the effect of sending the sufferer to sleep. If the tooth is so bad also another kind of liquid is put on it which makes it impossible for the patient to feel any pain in that particular spot.

74. One reason why there was so much suffering in past ages was that until one hundred years ago, nobody knew exactly how illness was causes. Two famous doctors found out a great deal about the cause of illness. (You can also do something in this your generation). They were Frenchman, Dr. Louis Pasteur who died in 1885, and a German, Dr. Kosh, who died in 1910. These two great men discovered that disease is caused by very tiny living things, colorless and transparent and so small that they cannot be seen with the eye alone. They are called germs. Although they are so small, they have

tails, and they can swim. Germs gets into people's blood and poison it, and so cause illness.

75. Pasteur discovered that each different disease is caused by a particular germ. There is one germ which causes malaria, another which causes consumption. Another for plague, and so on. Dr. Kosh inventers a method of colouring these tiny transparent creatures so that they could be seen through a microscope. The microscope has been a very great value to doctors in their study of germs. It is an instrument which magnifies small things many times so that they are made to appear larger than they really are. The microscope magnifies germs so much that they can be seen.

76. About one hundred and sixty years ago, an English doctor named Dr. Jenner notice that people who had an illness called cowpox never had the serious disease small pox. The tow diseases are somewhat similar, but the former generally attacks cows only. Human beings very rarely get it.

77. The latter is a very serious and painful illness. Probably you have been vaccinated against small pox. When the doctor vaccinated you, he put a small amount of cowpox vaccine into your arm. That has protected you from smallpox. By vaccination of that kind, many thousands of lives have been saved

78. Now, I am testing you on your concentration, and thinking level. But you will have to be faithful to yourself in order

to pass this examination. My examination is based on fundamental concentration and thinking. Remember to faithful to yourself.

79. Go to or look for a very quiet place or a room and hide yourself in there. Take a picture of yourself or something or someone who really you admire along. Now sit down if possible, like the Muslims or the Hindus usually do in their temple—sit in that position.

80. Now relax bring out your picture; and hold it in your hands. Forget about anything on this earth as though you are the only living thing on this planet earth. Forget about all your worries, cares, enemies, love ones, in-f act, forget off everything that you can think of, forget it! It may be difficult but use your intellect by deciding to forget off anything that may come across your mind that is not in line with your purpose!

81. Now, concentrate on your 'picture'. Think carefully of how beautiful the picture looks like. The position of the ear, nose, mouth, eyes, the colour of the dress, hair and the size and texture of the 'picture' and so on.

82. Congratulations! With persistent effort you have been able to do this with your undivided attention. If not keep on trying but maintaining that same position that you first started with. It is only loosers that stop trying when the going gets tough—winners never give up. It is not in them to give up

or quit. They keep trying by practicing with persistent effort until they become winners.

83. Refuse to give up, because quitters never win and winners never quit! They are convinced concerned, passionate, and they stay in the race, and this is the qualities of a person with true courage.

84. Now, set half an hour or an hour for practicing this exercise of concentration and thinking every day. When you practice it often, the conscious minds impresses the sub-conscious mind and when that is effected, concentration and thinking becomes your custom. The more you do this exercise, the more you develop your mental mind. Has it not been said: "A mall seed planted in a soil grows tall to become a big tree?" So it is with this mental exercise.

85. When you have mastered this, it means that, when you go to sleep, you are able to lie down on your bed and sleep immediately without difficulty of you having to think for a while before you are able to sleep. If you go to bed, and you think for a while before sleeping then you have not mastered yourself yet. You are not controlling yourself yet. I happened to get the chance to join a December retreat programme organize by the Deeper Life Church. The programme was an excellent one. I witnessed everything being done within time; in—fact, everybody there was time conscious. If all the people who went to the programme continued with this kind of life in their various communities, I personally

think a great change of life into a great improvement of the individual's life would be affected. They will be outstanding in their businesses, education, and every other aspect of their life should they continue with that kind of lifestyle.

86. Some people when they go to bed, now before all sort of thoughts come into their mind as if they are now closing their day's budget. They think for while, struggling with themselves to forget off their thinking and sleep. This is so because they are unable to schedule their time within (24) twenty-four hours a day. These individuals are unable to determine the day to their own advantage but rather their life is determined by the day instead.

87. Such individuals seem to forget that we live in a world where everything works within time, and that we are not now living in eternity. The day robs them off their own integrity. And the most amazing part is that there ore still some individuals who thinks that this is normal. Why has this become normal? Because we now live in an environment where fact and truth is a stranger than friction—what is abnormal becomes normal for lack of observation on things happening around us.

88. Build a house in your mind for me in one of your exercise. First, think or meditate on the land, the environment, the type of the building it will be. Think of the foundation of the building, how you will want the house the colour of painting that you will want in the building. How you will dress the inside for me—build a complete beautiful house

for me. If you have done it correctly, then, thanks for your gift. Remember that you must always be in the same position you first started comfortably with.

89. Again, come to think of it, you want to change your way of life or living, if good then for the better, thinking it positively. Thinking to create a new future for yourself. Making sure that your yes is yes, and no, no! Walking your talks and talking your walks—integrity. Being recognized as diligently mission concentrated person, and finally, making sure that all your targeted aims are achieved with love.

90. The Universal L aw is so advantageous that, it is not what you wish for in life that you will get but that which you have consciously or unconsciously thought of in your mind that sets into operation the law of attraction and then finally the results is come to pass. All the same if you speak forth your conscious or sub—conscious thoughts, you set forth the law of vibration which also set forth the law of attract into operation and then finally the result is come to pass. This is the modus-operandi of the Universal Law.

91. So speak forth the truth that you know, even the veriest little truths speak it forth for you are a ruler of many nations.

92. Wishes come to pass only in magical tales and movies. Chase after real power instead of shadow power.

CHAPTER 2

DISCOVER HOW TO ACT IN FAITH AND THINKING IN A CONSTRUCTIVE ACTION TO LEAD DISCIPLES

Abraham of Canaan, an ancestor of Israel thought hard and believed that God wanted him out of his fathers house to a land he did not know; but with faith he took the bold, courageous, and hopeful step, and the story goes on and on. Today, he is considered the father of many nations. Everybody in Christendom claims to be a descendant of Abraham, even in Islam; that is the faith you need.

1. It is you yourself that needs to discover your hidden talents with help in the Universal Law. You cannot do anything good outside the wonderfully designed laws under which we live, which are designed solely for our benefit or advantage. If you do something not within the laws, you are guilty and simply foolish.

2. This is mathematically true, this is under the topic known as Vectors—"The points E (-2,1), F(2,1), G(1,4), and H(a,b) are the vertices of a parallelogram EFGH. Find EF and GH and deduce the values of a and b".

3. Following or observing under the topic Vectors?

   a) EF= f-e= (2, 1)—(-2, 1) = (4, 0)
      GH= h-g = (1, 4)—(a, b) = (1-a, 4-b)
      Since EFGH is a parallelogram Ef = GH

   b) EF =GH (4, 0) = (1-a, 4-b)
      4 = 1-a→a = 1-4→a = -3
      0= 4-b→b = 4-0→b=4

   c)

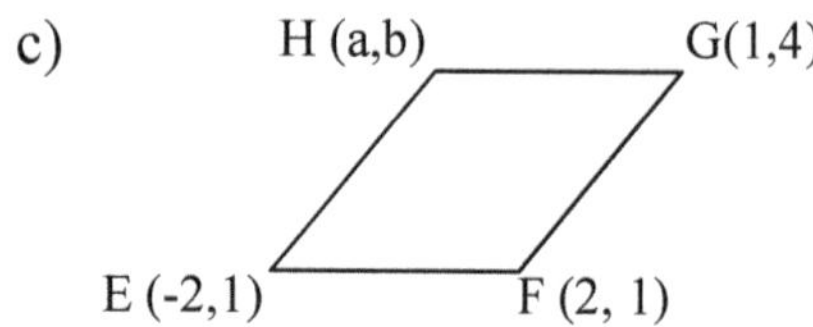

4. The hidden talent is now found to be (-3,4). It is you yourself that will have to search through your abilities and find out which one will be more useful to your environment and to you. You must take a step further in religion, science, and philosophy and look or see right within yourself for that hidden gift that you need to make the difference which is in you and no-where else. Just work through your little talents and you will discover them.

5. H (a,b) which was of no use, now has been discovered to be containing useful numbers as EF, and G-H (a,b)= H (-3,4). All that you need for life's success has been made available in the Universal Law.
   (I once read a work in my father's room where he loved to do his learning. In summary, the work said: "When things go wrong as they sometimes do, when the road you are trudging seems all up hill when the funds are low and the debts are high; and you want to smile but you have to sigh, when care is pressing you down a bit, rest if you must but do not you quit.")

6. Life is queer with its twist and turns, as everyone of us sometime learns and many a failure turns about when he might have won he stuck it out; so do not give up, though the pace seems slow—for you may succeed with another blow.

7. Often the goal is nearer than it seems to a fain and faltering man. Often the struggler has given up when he learned too late when the night slipped down how close he was to the golden crown.

8. Success is failure, turned inside out. The silver tint of the clouds of doubt. And you never can tell how close you are—when you live your life by heart—for it may be near when it seems afar and so stick to the fight when you are hardest hit, it is when things seem worst that you must not quit. Romans 8:38-39.

9. Did you know that . . . people do not accidentally stumble into failure, poverty or lack? They . . . think their way into it. He who does not encourage himself or hope to win has already lost whatever he intended to achieve. Defeat, failure, worries, just to mention but a few, never come to any man until he admits it. This is nothing but the truth. Making or causing you to have the mindset or mentality of a leader. Sometimes, I personally find it very difficult to accept it when someone tells me that: 'I am poor; I do not have money to buy even food today'. Whilst maybe the younger brother may be considered to be rich in that society. What was his attitude years back, and that of his brother?

10. The difference must certainly be . . . their mindset. Attitude when calculated, add or sum up, is exactly one hundred per cent (100%). This brings to mind another issue, he the elder one is not a correct thinker as the younger one—he lacks courage, hope or faith and vice versa the younger one.

(A	B	C	D	E	F	G	H	I	J
K	L	M	N	O	P	Q	R	S	T
U	V	W	X	Y	Z				
↓	↓	↓	↓	↓	↓	↓	↓	↓	↓
↓	↓	↓	↓	↓	↓	↓	↓	↓	↓
↓	↓	↓	↓	↓	↓				
1	2	3	4	5	6	7	8	9	10
11	12	13	14	15	16	17	18	19	20
21	22	23	24	25	26				

Every word can be calculated mathematically using this fundamental principle of an alphabet mapping a number. Thus the word ATTITUDE when calculated equals one hundred percent mathematically.

ATTITUDE=	A	+	T	+	T	+	I	+	T	+	U	+	D	+	E	=
ATTITUDE=	100%															
	↓		↓		↓		↓		↓		↓		↓		↓	
	1	+	20	+	20	+	9	+	20	+	21	+	4	+	5	

In your characteristics, attitude should be your greatest priority. It should come first before any other priority—faith, courage and so on. Because faith, courage, truth and so on without an attitude is dangerous, and none of these or other word equals one hundred percent. So watch you attitude very carefully.

Human beings only catch 50% as their maximum when it comes to attitude, while most of them say, 92% fall below the 50% mark. All other words can be calculated using the same example as I have done with ATTITUDE.)

11. To be a leader, you have to make people want to follow you, and nobody wants to follow someone who does not know where he is going. The blind cannot lead the blind. When a wise person speaks, everyone is silent and they hail or praise him to the skies for what he says. But let the opposite of the wise man speak—the one who lives a reckless life—that is, everybody says "who is that?" though they may know him

or " do not take him seriously." Why? Because he is simply foolish. You must be able to construct good things out of the bad or out of nothing, and I am not talking of absolutely nothing. Because out of absolutely nothing, nothing comes.

12. Do you want to know whether you are truly destined to be successful leader? If yes. Then let us find out. The test is simple and basic and factual. Find out what you are already doing to the person working under you or the one you are serving now. Is uses the end product of your authority or services? Are you sacrificing yourself for them, even your very self? Are you consciously conscious of being in time and not on time? If you examine yourself, and the answer is no! then I am sorry because of you, forget it, and simply drop out. But if yes, then the earth on which you walk is rejoicing under you and also I salute you my lord! For surely you will be great leader.

13. A good leader assumes the best in people instead of the worst, and is a generational thinker and not seeking for his own interest alone. He always finds a way to do the impossible to bring joy upon his followers. Set backs does not stop him from where is going or what he intends to achieve on behalf of his followers.

14. Abraham Lincoln had so many setbacks in his political career but he still rose to move a nation, and helped free a people—the slaves, and a divided nation—freeing slaves, and making one nation out of divided one.

15. Such people inspire in their subjects to achieve whatever lawful thing they set their mind to do with respect to the Universal Law which is their basic importance on earth. Disciples need someone with a good idea, and can take a risk which will benefit them (disciples), and start a new achievable project such as businesses, and so on.

16. He is not afraid to die for them. Fear is totally out of his minds' dictionary. The very thought of death is bitter to someone who is prosperous, living peacefully with his wealth, free from worries, and still able to enjoy his food. But this is not so with a great leader. He is not afraid of death's decree because he knows and understands that it came to those before him and will come to those after him. The law has ruled it in the mental world for every living creature; and who can object to that which is from the Universal Law? He knows and understand also that, in the world of the dead no one will care whether you lived ten years, a hundred or a thousand, but the question will be what life did you live on earth? And so, will fight to defend his followers when the time calls for that purpose—Love in itself.

17. There are some individuals who will become leaders and other will not. Why? Because of the mind—the mind differentiates every individual—their understanding and actions.

18. When leaders go before their God to talk to him, they ask for (9,9,9) nine, nine, nine which are in long life. Peace, grace, and favors; success, victory, and prosperity; wisdom, knowledge

and understanding, but the ordinary ask for (6,6,6) six, six, six, unconsciously. The application of wisdom, knowledge, and understanding is far from them—they ask the vice versa of peace, grace, and favor; success, victory, and prosperity either consciously or unconsciously. Because they lack wisdom, knowledge and understanding, automatically they lack peace, grace, favor; success, victory and prosperity. In their quest for what they lack, they accept their ignorance and find themselves living in a state of misery—hell.

19. There are some individuals wanting to be rulers of organizations, but keep on hurting others instead of being of positive impact on them—helping those they think can be of great benefit to them, and oppressing the poor or needy. A good master loves, and loves even his oppressors, loving his enemies and hating what makes them his enemies such as ideological factors, and so on. No great leader will suffer a set of people or group for their ideological differences such as: " I will suffer this group or set of people for on the day of battle they were not on my side". Overcoming this problem has made Professor John Evans Fiifi Atta Mills, and John Agyekum Kufour, all former presidents of Ghana, they have become geniuses and example for younger generations to learn from.

20. Never be happy if all are on your side. It will make you relax—lazy in thinking and this brings about less improvement.

21. Good leaders know that they must help their converts, feed, assist them in every way that they can—if they want to see a prosperous organization, nation, and so on. An ignorant leader is a bad leader, and vise versa. A good leader is skilful in managing scarce resources. He thinks, and talks positively, and everything about him shall be positive, and he never resists changes, for it shall always come.

    (Considering a good farmer, he knows that he must help his soil, feed his plants, and assist nature in every way that he can, if he wants to reap a good harvest at the end of the year. The more a farmer knows, the better his crops will be. An ignorant farmer is usually a bad farmer, working so hard for little produce. This is no different in philosophy, and religion.)

22. There is not a single person anywhere in the world who is not capable of doing more than he thinks he can. Remember, it is what you think, and do that makes you who you are. For a man is what he thinks he is. Even in religion, God told the Israelites people that: "what ever you think I am, that is what I am", and he is the "I am". This is no different. Your right train of thoughts will take you to the right station in life.

23. Man is not man from his face or from his speech but rather, man is man from his understanding, and will. It is this understanding, and will that bring out the qualities in a man, inspires him to become a leader. A man may have the ability to teach but still not be of much use to himself. He may be

clever with words, but end up starving because people hate him.

24. An individual may consider himself wise and let you know that he is certain about what he knows. A man who really is wise will be the teacher of his people, and they can be certain that what he teaches is the truth. Everyone will praise such a person and speak of him as fortunate. A person's life has only a limited number of days, but the life of a country cannot be measured in days at all. A wise man will win the confidence of his people, and they will remember him for ever.

25. Repeated victories over your problems are the rungs on your ladder to success. With each victory you grow in wisdom, stature, and experience. You become a better, wiser, and more successful person each time you meet a problem, and tackle, and conquer it with a positive mental attitude.

26. Making a constructive plan in life is like working a mathematical problem especially, working under the topic 'Construction'.

27. When you want to construct an angle of 45° at a point 'B', you first have to construct an angle of 90°, and then you bisect it to get the required angle. The same applies to constructing an angle of 22 ½, you first construct an angle of 90° then you bisect it to get an angle 45°, then the 45° is also bisected to get an angle of 22 ½ which is the final destination. You do

not just jump over what must be done first to doing the last. This is not how the principles of the Universal Law operate. Others may have been ahead of you in life because they started their construction works early before you or they are applying the rightful principles.

(Sometimes, my friends do ask me this question: "Hey! You this guy, you are smart in life, why?" this has always been my answer: "I am not that smart as you think but it is that, I do stay longer with a problem to know the root cause of it, tackle, and solve it once, and forever.)

28. If you have tried your hands at something and failed, the next thing is to try your head. Thinking will get you to the bottom of the problem and faith or courage will get you to the top. In other words, I mean, thinking will get you to the starting point of your discovery, and faith or courage or being courageous will make you possess your discovery.

29. If you must be a champion, then, as the truth is chase after real power instead of shadow power, wealth instead of riches, honour instead of fame, and finally service instead of position.

30. Live your life as simple as you are. Do not do what others say, just listen to them, but do what you feel is good with respect to the Law. Do not go on brand name; just wear those things in which you feel comfortable. Do not waste your money on unnecessary things; just spend on them who are

really in need rather. After all it is your life then why gives chance to others to rule your life.

31. Be a unique person knowing your abilities. Why? Because truly that is what you are. What? You have got a unique name that no body else in the world have got and many other things.

32. Being wise is better than being strong; yes knowledge is more important than strength. After all, you must make careful plans before you fight a battle which can be an examination or sports contest, and so on. The more good advice you get, the more likely you are to win. (Proverb 24:5).

33. A very good prosperous destined leader inculcate the habit of buying brand new products or goods. This then, when followed creates employment. Because the manufacturer is able to manufacture more for the market, and employees get paid, stay in business and so on.

34. When more people buy original (brand-new) products, production increases, and more and more people are employed. The economy becomes favorable. Because workers are able to pay or cater for their basic necessities needed to make life comfortable.

35. On the other hand, when the individual is encouraged to buy the so called second-hand (used) products, there is massive unemployment. Why? Because, the products that

the workers produce are not being bought and the effect is that, employees (workers) are layed off work. Life becomes difficult for them to handle. There is massive poverty in the environment due to consumers demand for supply being low. This mounts up all kinds of social vices. This is a fact, in economics especially under employment and unemployment theory. A good economist can detail you on this truth.

36. A person without faith or being courageous in the Universal Law and himself cannot survive. Such a mind is not a surviving mind. When you lose hope or courage of doing better, you lose everything that makes life worth living. Remember that, all truly wise thoughts have been thought already, long ago, thousands of time, and millions of years, but to make them truly ours, we must think them over again honesty till they take root in our personal experiences.

(Think about the United States of America, the most powerful nation in the world now. They decide who to help. The seed of success is in them, that is the truth. They know how to save large amount of gold reserves, oil reserves, just to mention but a few. Great Britain or England as we know is a small country, probably an Island. Ghana in West Africa is bigger than England. Great Britain is about the size of Ghana. But in London alone, there are three times as many people, living there as there are in the whole of Ghana. Great Britain thought hard to become an industrial country–most of the people work in mines and factories, making things to sell–Great Britain. Now come think of Great Britain.

The whole of the United States of America was built by this small land mass country−Great Britain. In short, U.S.A is a product of England. Everything has source or a cause. Correct thinking makes all things possible.)

37. This is another great story of Abraham Lincoln born in 1809-1865 was a great philosopher and a leader. His hometown was in a little log cabin in the state of Kentucky, in the United States of America, His father was a poor farmer and from his babyhood, Abraham had help on the farm. At the local school he learned to read, and write but not much more.

38. In his home there were books which he read over and over again. They were three of the best books in the world probably then—the Bible, Aesop's Fables, and Bunyan's Pilgrims Progress and young Abraham learned them almost by heart. He loved reading and when he got older he spent almost every penny he had on buying books.

39. He earned his living in various ways. At one point he traded, at another he worked in the village store in the village near his home. In his spare time he studied Law, and he soon made a name for himself as an honest, clever, and trustworthy young man. The ignorant farmers in the district often used to come to him for advice and help in their difficulties.

40. He was always interested in politics and began to think he would like to take part in the government of the state of

Illinois where he lived. When he was twenty-five (25), he was elected a member of the Illinois House of Representatives. He worked and represented the people so well that for eight years they regularly re-elected him every time there was an election. They came to trust him so much that in the end they chose him to represent them in the Congress of the United States of America in Washington. So the young back wood boy rose to become a member of congress with a hand in the Government of his country.

41. He was still working as a lawyer in Springfield, the capital of Illinois and he might never have become world-famous man if it had not been for the question of slavery. There were many slaves in the Southern States of America, working on the cotton plantations and their owners all thought they would be ruined if slavery came to an end.

42. But in the Northern States, there were no cotton plantations and the people there wanted to follow the examples of Great Britain and do away with slavery. Among them was Stephen Douglas and when he came to Springfield to make speeches in defense of slavery it was young Abraham Lincoln who stood up, and answered him so cleverly that he won all the people at the meeting over to his side.

43. Lincoln had left congress after one year but now he stood for election again as Douglas' opponent, and when he was forty-nine he was chosen to be a senator of the United States.

The struggle over slavery went on for many years and always Lincoln stood up for the freeing of the slaves.

44. At last when he was fifty-four (54) there was a tremendous struggle between Lincoln and Douglas, when both were standing for the Presidential elections in America. In the end Lincoln was elected and became the President of the United States of America.

45. The slave-owners now knew that one of the first thing Lincoln would do would be to get a law passed forbidding slavery. So the Southern States, where the slaves were, decided to break away form the Northern States, and form a separate slave-owing country of their own.

46. Everybody waited to see what Lincoln would do. He knew that, if the Southern States were allowed to break away there would be no hope of stopping slavery there for many years. So he said that the Southern States had no right to break away and if necessary the Northern States would go to war to keep them in the union.

47. So the American Civil War began. It lasted for four years. Thousands of Americans were killed, towns were burnt, and farms destroyed, and there was a great deal of suffering. Fortunately the Northern States had a very clever general called Ulysses Grant, and it was due to his clever leadership that in the end the Southern States were defeated, and the

United States of America remained one instead of being divided into two.

48. As soon as the war was over in the very same year a law was passed in America, freeing all slaves in the United States, and forbidding slavery within the Union for ever.

49. Lincoln did not live long to see the peace he had so badly wanted. A few weeks after peace had been signed, he went to the theatre with his wife to see a play. An actor, who was half-mad, and who believed that Lincoln was an evil man, crept into the president box and shot Lincoln through the back of the head and he died within a few minutes.

50. Lincoln was a very great man. One of his secretaries wrote of him: 'There is no man in the country so wise, so gentle, and so firm! He was full of selfless love for America and for its people. They gave him the nickname of "Honest Abe," because even his enemies knew him to be a man they could trust, and one who was really given up to the service of his country.

51. Abraham's own aims are summed up in a speech he made when he was president, at the dedication of a burial-growing at Gettysburg for soldiers who had died in the Civil War. His speech ended with these words "We here resolve that these dead shall not have died in vain, that this nation, under God, shall have a new birth of freedom, and thus government of

the people, by the people, for the people, shall not perish from the earth".

52. In reality leadership is like walking on water or driving successful on a very bad road. We are all aware that not every driver can drive well on bad roads. It takes more than a desire or will to do that. Preparations and a very sound knowledge of the route are equally important. Very fatal accidents may occur when even potholes are ignored, not to mention the danger of protruding rocks on such roads.

53. Whether one leads a large business unit, a school or a small group on a corner somewhere, success requires an up to date knowledge of the things that can derail a leader. It is only when leaders know where to step, and diligently execute their responsibilities that they can make a very positive impact.

54. In some countries the inability even of business leaders to achieve targets attracted sanctions. Such countries made some scapegoats to show that leadership is neither a tea party, a pleasure trip, recreational ground, nor a place for personal aggrandizement.

55. It is an issue of uttermost importance. It is a fact that in China, poor performance is dealt with in a much more hostile manner. A scenario is in the mid 1980's a Chinese newspaper reported that eighteen factory managers were executed for poor quality at Chien Bien. Refrigerator factory on the outskirt of Beijing. The managers—12 men, and six

women—were taken to a rice paddy outside the factory, and unceremoniously shot to death while 500 plant workers looked on.

56. Also “in 1985 pravada newspaper reported that three female factory managers were sentenced to two years in a labour camp, and fined $14,000 for producing poor quality clothes at a government factory, and in addition, they were fined 20 percent of all future salaries.

57. These are extreme cases, and although this book is not advocating similar actions, it is time leaders stepped up their responsibilities to improve the lives of the groups they lead, and the quality of whatever they produce. If you want to succeed, and continue to stay at the top, pay attention to the following “steps” which several leaders strongly recommend will enable you to walk on the “Leadership water”. You know what? Have very high ethics, and energy. Be enthusiastic, goal-oriented, hardworking, courageous, priority-driven, level-headed. Consistent, and dedicated to developing, and seeing to the welfare of your followers. Be rest assured that ethics is as infectious as measles, and if you set good examples your subordinates are more likely to learn from you, and spread the message.

58. It is important for every leader to be credible. Loyalty of our followers derives from credibility. Bonuses, sanctions, and salary increases will not do it. Remember that credibility builds trust, and trust builds loyalty. If followers are not loyal,

only a close, open sincere personal relationship between you and your team will do it.

59. This is the relationship you have to have in the Universal Law. Leaders often inadvertently destroy their own credibility. This is a typical illustrations which are the half truths they trade, blatant lies they tell, the divided-and-rule tactics they employ coupled with fear, and inability to take decisions, and act.

60. Endeavour to let your followers grasp you objectives, and sense of directions well. People who are good, and will want to really work for results will not be happy just muddling through or working aimlessly.

61. In setting out your objectives, make them know that you welcome ideas, and that no idea is too insignificant to be considered, and avoid unnecessary bureaucracy. If you are bureaucratic, people will find you to be very slow, boring, incapable of taking decisions, and unproductive.

62. Also endeavour not to be a stooge or bootlicker. Followers will lose confidence in you if they become aware that you cannot stand for them or stand for the truth. Have a dream, study diligently, plan, take action and continuously look for more stones on which to stand to succeed.

63. Every youth in Ghana is encouraged to know this song, and meditate upon it. “Arise Ghana youth for your country. Your

nation demands your devotion. Let us all unite to uphold her and make her strong. We are all involved, in building our fathers' land."

64. It is their heritance, and it is a must obligation to which they must not escape, if they want improvement in their land. Maybe this is what is brought about the peace in the country seeing everybody in the country as one nation—be it a foreigner or a citizen; tribe or clan; and whatever religious group one may be from.

65. Remember that, whatever positive thing that you intend to create, do it! And when it is not as successful as you would have wanted it, try again. Know and understand that, Thomas Edison, the man who invented Light bulb, tried it over again, and again, and again until he was successful in his determination to invent, and impact positively on his environment by effecting a light bulb. Do not allow negative thought from people around to distract you from your purpose. This is what is known as thinking local, and acting global. Today, his invention has affected you and I positively.

66. You can do something if not a likeness of what he has done. You can do something unique in the business world.

67. This is a constructive plan of someone in the business world who is been so successful. He had a long term plan—a view of where he was going, how he was going to get there—his

mission, and how he will know if he gets there. So he designed ways of reaching there—again that is his mission.

68. The mission served as a check point to him—he never uses his money capital or asset by heart. Every business money that went out went to the right place, and was to bring benefit to the business. He does not involves himself in an unprofitable friendship, idling, and was punctual at his business; well focused; not wasting time but was time conscious. He did not spend because others were spending. He spend because his business demands so.

69. One thing was his greatest support—he 'loved' saving his money with the bank for security purpose, and he was guaranteed of the safety of his money. One of the good books was his greatest consultant in his business.
(The Bible, Koran, Holy Shiva Purana, offers a constructive counsel on how a youth or an individual can improve their lives. the truth in them can give to the inexperienced ones shrewdness, to a young man knowledge, and thinking ability. Just consider how their principles can help.)

70. His vision was to set-up a purified water manufacturing company—in (5) five years time. He began with the sales of one-by-one out of one sachet bag, then to the sales of the sachets itself, then became a distributor, then finally, he established his vision—the purified water manufacturing company.

71. His beginning was not that of a proud one to boast about but remember, he who dares to fail greatly can achieve greatly. If you refuse to bow before the king, then he will in place not honour you. You cannot want to go to heaven without dying first. If that happens then you must have already had a luxurious inheritance to tap into it.

72. The foolishness of the Universal Law is wiser than men; and the weakness of the Universal Law is stronger than men. Read in first Corinthians 1:25 in the bible.
(This "1 Corinthians 1:25" was speaking primarily about the cross. The cross was the weakest and most foolish thing that you could conceive of in the culture of that time, but out of the weakness of the cross came the almightiness of God. Out of the foolishness of the cross came the unsearchable wisdom of God. So some times, we have to go to something very weak and foolish to receive God's wisdom and strength. This is the "Number Law"—the law of number counting—0, 1, 2, 3 to infinity.)

73. Do this exercise for me in the night. Lie down in a quite open place with your back on the floor or ground; and with your face facing the sky. Relax as though you are about to sleep.

74. Forget off any other thing that you can think of—worries, cares, happiness, excitement, and whatever thing that you can think of or may come across your mind. What is needed now is your total concentration, an undivided attention.

75. Think as though you have been blind throughout your years on earth, and this is your very first time of having your eyesight and there is no human being around you to explain anything to you.

76. Now you are challenged to find out the 'cause' of everything that the greedy eye can now see! Remember how you started with the first test or examination in chapter one. But this time on, you are like sleeping with your back facing the floor or ground. This exercise can be done in your own room using the things in your room to think.

77. Now think quietly of how the clouds are moving in the sky. How some are big, and some small in sizes. Think of the pace in which they move to cover the star making the star invisible, and then moving away to make it visible again.

78. Think of the distance from the ground to the sky, and the hugeness of the sky; the shape of the moon, that is, if it is visible to you. Now think of the thing that brought about all these things. Think of the authority or wisdom of that thing. What laws are there that governs all these creation.

79. Now think of the cause of these effects that you are now seeing all around you. Can you hear the sound of silent living things around you such as trees; the sounds in silence? Close your eyes and listen to these silent sounds. Open it again, and think of the beauty of the sky; the beauty of silence.

Think of the causes and the laws that govern them in their activities.

80. Observe very closely like the cat or lion the rational of these observations. Can you think to create to make something out of these observations all around you? Think, do something creative, and very good, because you are a unique person with unique qualities to think to affect your community, state, region or your country. Think about these things and do something unique for your community, state, region or country—something honorable.

81. Do something for the world and the glory bounces back to you. Do not beg. If you have to depend on someone else for your food; you are not really living your own life. You pollute yourself of any sensitive person. A shameless person can make begging sound sweet, but something inside him or her burns. You are a thinker, and so, you are the one suppose to give more than to receive.

CHAPTER 3

ALL CREATED THINGS OF EFFECTS ARE FROM A CAUSE WHICH IS THE UNIVERSAL LAW

With this wisdom, knowledge, and understanding, you will freely worship in your inner man, and become a blessing to generations yet unborn. Your blessing will endure until the moon is no more. From the ends of the world, your discoveries will be useful, even unto eternity. You will become a god and act as God. You will do things as though from your own self. Your legend will be the unforgotten story that many will gather to listen to and learn from, for the beautification of the mind, religiously, scientifically, and philosophically. You will become the Guru that your descendants will love to practice.

A scholar must have time to study if he is going to be wise, he must be relieved of other responsibilities.

1. How can a farmhand gain knowledge, when his only ambition is to drive the oxen and make them work, when all he is able to talk about is livestock? He takes great pains to plough a straight furrow and will work far into the night to feed the animals.

2. It is the same with the artist, and the craftsman who work night and day engraving precious stones, carefully working out new designs. They take great pains to produce a lifelike image and will work far into the night to finish the work.

3. Can you imagine the blacksmith at his anvil, planning what he will make from a piece of iron. The heat from the fire sears his skin as he sweat away at the forge. The clanging of the hammer deafens him as he carefully watches the object he is working with, take shape. He takes great pains to complete his task, and will work far into the night to bring it to perfection.

4. What about the potter? Sitting at his wheel, and work concerned with how many objects he can produce. He works the clay with his feet, until he can shape it with his hands; then he takes great pains to glaze it properly and will work far into the night to clean out the kiln.

5. Even the shoemaker; all these people are skilled with their hands each of them an expert at his own craft. Without such people there could be no cities; no one would live or visit where these services were not available.

(If someone travels to your hometown—in the village to do business or trade, do not look down on him or her, but rather be appreciative, and not abusive. Because, it is due to life's struggle that is bought him or her there. If not, he or she is also gotten at least something in his or her village where he or she comes from)

6. These people are not sought out to serve on the public councils, and they never attain position of great importance. They do not serve as lawyers, judges, and do not understand legal matters. They have no education and are not known for their wisdom. You never hear them quoting proverbs. But the work they do holds this world together. When they do their work, it is the same as offering prayers. Because they are very useful; and 'use, is performing one's duty of office well is the fundamental of 'use', but I will define it at the end of this work.

7. But this is different with the person who devotes himself to studying about the Universal Law. He examines the wisdom of all the ancient writers and concerns himself with the prophecies. He studies the hidden meanings of proverbs, and is able to discuss the obscure points of parables. For instance, 'King Solomon' and 'the Queen of Sheba' is a typical illustration which can be found in the Bible.

8. Great people call on him for his service and he is seen in the company of rulers. He travels to foreign lands in his efforts to learn about human good and evil. It is his practice to get up

early and pray and meditate on the Universal Law, seeking his faults and changing them to his advantage—asking God to forgive his sins. Then if God—in religion is willing he will be filled with understanding.

9. He will pour out a stream of wise sayings and give thanks to his creator in prayer. He will have knowledge to share and good advice to give as well as insight into the arcana's of the Universal Law. He will be widely praised for his wisdom, and he will never be lost because people for generations to come will remember him.

10. Now, there are some individuals who believe that to live the life that leads to heaven is difficult. Why? They have been told that man must renounce the world, resist its lusts usually the lusts of the body, and the flesh, must live spiritually—in religion.

11. They understand this to mean that they must discard worldly things which consist chiefly in riches, wealth and honour. These one's are told to walk continually in spiritual meditation on the Universal Law, usually called GOD in religion, and must spend their life in prayers and in reading about the 'Word' and spiritual books. This is become their idea of renouncing the world, living in the spirit; not in the flesh.

12. Those who renounce the world, and live in the spirit in this manner acquire a sorrowful life that is not receptive of joy

that the Universal Energy gives. You must understand that everyone's life continues the same after death. Because death is not a definite end of man as some do think and say.

13. To be able to enjoy the life that the Universal Law gives, you must employ yourself into the Universal Energy, and participate in the Universal Principle in the world—in its business, and employments. But remember to act on good conscience towards your neighbour.

14. The importance of all religion, science, and philosophy is to acknowledge the Universal Law, and desist from evil practices.

15. Truly, you can live outwardly as others do. You can grow fabulously, and famously rich, live in an extravagant houses, wear designer nice clothing according to your conditions and functions; enjoy delights and engage in worldly affairs for the sake of your occupation, business, and for the life both of the mind, and body, provided you inwardly acknowledge the Universal Law, and wish your neighbour well—(the individual next to you)

16. Interestingly, the way to heaven is not so difficult as many believe. The fundamental difficulty that needs to be over-come lies in resisting the love of self and the world; to close their becoming dominate in you. For they are the cause of all and all evils.

17. Both good, and bad individuals enjoy honour and possessions; yet the good individual destines himself to heaven. Being wealthy in riches, honour and possessions contain both blessings and curses. Blessings to the good individual and cusses to the bad individuals.

18. With the understanding of the Universal Law, you will notice that in heaven itself, there are both rich and poor, great and small and the same applies in hell. The individual who set his heart upon his possessions is the cursed, and vice versa.

19. Has it not been said:—' The starting point of all accomplishment is desire that the law makes room for an individual with purpose. The pursuit of excellence is the passion of all achievers. Your vision well planned is a preview to your greatness. Therefore do not let anybody steal your dream or vision.

20. Man is creating and improving every second, every minute, every hour, and every day! It is man through the Universal Law that create, re-create, make, and improve on everything that you see all around you. Creativity is pure mathematical formula, in-fact, methodical that you must not escape it. This is pure science that brings about inventory. It is faith in the Universal Law that brings about answers or miracles. Miracles are themselves so to us, because of our lack of understanding of the things that happens in the mental world.

    (Jesus of Nazareth applied himself into the laws or law. He knew that he had acted within the laws of the Universal, but his op-posers were acting outside the laws. And so he was able to encourage his disciples to have courage, for he was convinced of justice. He was certain that justice will prevail. Why? Because all of his actions were done within the context of the Universal Law. So when judgment was pronounced, he was victorious, and it was evident to them that uphold justice. Nobody acts within the laws of the constitution of his state or country and is punished for that or pronounced guilty of wrong doing. If so, then, justice have not been served or done. The truth is that injustice happens in a corruptible country, but that is not the case with the Universal Law.)

21. Imagination is the fundamental tool to inventory. First the object is held in the mind, then development rains on it while the object is still in the mind. Inventors, leaders, and business successful individuals have this principle well developed and applied.

22. The inventor before he begins with his invention, the image of the object, design or plan is consciously held in his mind. He develops it in the mind, tackles all the advantages, and disadvantages very carefully. He builds the whole object, design or plan or idea in his mind till completion—from the foundation till the end. Making sure that every addition, subtraction, multiplication, and so on that needs to be made are correctly done in his or her conscious mind first, and then it becomes part of his or her sub—conscious thought.

23. Then he puts his imaginations on paper then into work. This is no different from the way that Moses gave the "Ten Commandments" to the Israelites. This is fundamental or basic principle, and should be known to every human individual. This is how God in religion created, and made man. Man is one of God's inventions.

24. This is my Krypton gift to you. So rise up from your dark universe or world, and do something attractive with the Krypton gift that you are now having. This is not about your age, but what you can do with the truth.

25. Remember, use it for a good cause for a wonderful result. "In the beginning Allah created this and that"—is a fact known in religion.

26. Religion brings to my mind the story of Christianity and Islam which I have personally read before over and over again for several times. And with your standard in concentration, let me tell you the stories.

27. Now, to begin with Christianity, there is a small country just north of Egypt along the sea coast called Palestine. In it there lived a people called the Jews. They had had a very sad time. For the great kings of Babylon and of Egypt often marched across their country and fought against them. Their chief city was destroyed and they were carried away captive to Babylon.

28. After a time a few came back and built their city again. But they still had an unhappy time, and at last the Romans made Palestine a part of their Empire and sent a governor there. The Jews always longing for the day when they should be free again and have a King of their own.

29. One day soon after the Romans had seized the land a little boy was born in Palestine called Jesus. He grew up as a carpenter's son and as he got older all men wondered at his goodness and wisdom.

30. When he became a man he spent his time going about doing good, and healing the sick and teaching people about God. Many followed him gladly. Some of the leaders of the Jews were jealous of his power. They brought him before the Roman Governor, and accused him of plotting to make himself King of the Jews. So the Governor had him executed.

31. The leaders of the Jews were glad to get rid of him. But his followers believed that he had risen from the dead and came to comfort them. They worshipped Jesus as the Son of God and began openly to preach their good news.

32. At first men laughed at them and the leaders of the Jews had them punished. Yet when people saw what good lives these men lived, and how their faith strengthened them, others too began to believe in Jesus. These people were called Christians.

33. These early followers of Jesus met together and planned to go out through the Roman Empire telling men about their Master. One of the chiefs of these travelers was called Paul. He was often thrown into prison by the Romans for his work. At last he was taken to Rome itself, and lived there for several years teaching men about Jesus. Then the Romans executed him because he would not pay honour to the Emperor as a god.

34. Gradually the Christian faith spread right through the Roman Empire. At first it was mainly the poor people who listened, and became Christians. Then others too were interested, until at last, after 300 years the Emperor Constantine himself become a Christian and tried to make Christianity the religion of the whole Empire (And the fact of the dates is that: Death of Jesus, A.D. 30; Constantine allows Christian worship A.D. 313)

35. Then soon after the Roman Empire fell a new Empire arose, which in some ways was just as wonderful. It was built up by the Arabs who were fired by the new religion of Islam. Here is the story of how it happened.

36. Arabia is very big country and much of it is desert land. There the Arabs lived as nomands, moving from well to well. And great caravans of camels went across the desert carrying dates and goods from other cities. Many Arabs lived in cities of which the chief was Mecca, but they were often fighting against each other.

37. Now in Mecca there was born a small boy named Mohammad. His uncle was a merchant who dealt in camels. As Muhammad grew up he learnt to help his uncle. And he also went to the temple called Kaaba, where he saw a great black stone the people worshipped—as well as more than 350 images of different gods!

38. Mohammad often thought about this, and he heard about the religion of the Christians and of the Jews. The more he 'thought' the more he believed that there was only one God over all the world, and that all men should worship Him. He believed that he Mohammed was the chosen Prophet of the true God, called in Arabic, Allah.

39. So Muhammad told some friends of this and they believed him. But when the people of Mecca heard of it, at first they laughed at Mohammad. They then became angry, and threw stones at him and drove him from the city. So Muhammad with his friends fled away to another city called Medina. This happened in the year A.D. 622. And the Mohammedans always count their dates from this year, just as Christians do from the birth of Jesus.

40. In Medina they built a small house of prayer, called a mosque. And the people of the city listened to Mohammad and believed his teaching.

41. Then the people of Medina fought against the men of Mecca and defeated them. The people of Mecca said they would

accept this new religion called Islam, if Muhammad would come back and live in their city. For they wanted Mecca still to be a sacred city, so that pilgrims would continue to visit it.

42. So Mohammad went back to Mecca and destroyed all images in the Kaaba and built a beautiful mosque instead. For he thought that God was so great that no man should presume to make an image of Him. The prophets Muhammad conquered all Arabia and all the Arabs followed Islam. And he sent messages to the kings of the earth, to Persia and China and many different lands urging them to accept Islam.

43. And then Mohammed died. But his followers were strong men and Arabian armies marched out and conquered many other countries. They took Palestine and Persia and Iraq. They came through the Himalayas into Northern India. They seized Egypt and marched right along the northern coast of African. They crossed into Spain and conquered it.

44. But they were stopped in France by a King called Charles who defeated them in a fierce battle. He was nicknamed "The Hammer" because of his great victory. And when the Arabs tried to cross from Asia Minor into Europe the great city of Constantinople defeated them. These wars took about 100 years.

45. Now wherever the Arabs went men accepted Islam. And everywhere they built beautiful mosques in which the Faithful could say their prayers. But the Muslim Empire did

not remain one state like the Roman Empire. It quickly broke up into many different kingdoms.

46. The Arabs took all the learning of the different cities which they conquered, and wrote it down in Arabic. As such, much of the learning of the Greeks was preserved by the Arabs. And they added much to it themselves. Them invented algebra and studied mathematics very deeply.

47. They were excellent doctors, and could perform very skilful operations and used medicine which sent their patients to sleep. They built lovely palaces and mosques, using graceful arches and bright-coloured tiles. And in these mosques were schools and universities too.

49. The Arabs built many fine cities, in Iraq they founded Bagdad. Most of you know the story of the great ruler of Bagdad, Harun al Rashid and how he had the Arabian Nights Entertainments written down. In that story we see the wealth of that great city in his days. Then the Arabs founded Cairo, the new city on the Nile, which is still the capital of Egypt. There the famous University of Al Azar still has students from all over the world.

50. In Spain their greatest city was Cordova which had one-third of a million people in it, and many mosques and palaces

50. Wherever the Muslims live, you see the mosque and hear the muezzin call to prayer at eventide, "God is great, There is no God but God, Muhammad is His Prophet"

52. Now in our next meditation exercise, you are now going to think of these two religions to figure out their common goals. Think of their belief in one God.

53. Muhammad's teachings were like those of the Jews and Christians, and he taught his followers to honour the Jewish prophets and Jesus. He also taught people to honour their parents, to be kind and thoughtful towards others to eat and drink wisely, and pray to God five times daily with their faces turned towards Mecca.
    (I want my readers to know and understand that hundred years later, after the death of the prophet Muhammad, the Arabs fought and successfully conquered outside countries like the Persia (Iran) in A.D. 637, Palestine (Israel) in A.D. 638, Egypt in A.D. 641 and so on. The Arab Muslims ruled in each country and people who were not Arabs were allowed to keep their own way, but had to pay tribute to their Arab rulers. And soon, something happened; many of the people who were not Arabs also became Muslims, because they found it easy to accept the religion of their new masters. Therefore, the Arabs conquests caused Islam to spread in many countries outside Arabia).

54. With this knowledge let us not forget that it is equally important to know what to avoid or what not to do as what

to do in the struggle for life. Knowing what not to do is like working mathematics in number base, the base in which you are working is what guilds you to your answer—(3215-1235) = 1435. the law for working this out is definite and you cannot escape from it and the knowledge can be understood best reading from one of the good books (Bible) in 2 Timothy 2:15-26.

(As you go through life, be-careful to keep your appetite under control, and do not eat anything that you know is bad for you. All food does not agree with everyone. And not everyone does, yes! like the same kind of food. Do not feel that you just have to have all sorts of fancy food, and do not be a glutton over any food. If you eat too much, you will always have stomach trouble and do not drink too much of soft drinks or alcohol.

54. This is able to make you wise for re-generation through faith or the base as in the above instance—the base inspires, protects you profitably for wisdom, knowledge and understanding and for reproof, correction, instruction in a constructive action in order to master your own destiny.

CHAPTER 4

KNOWING TOTAL OR WHOLE TRUTH FROM HALF OR FALSE TRUTH

In this chapter, I am expliciting on the word 'Faith'. After this constrictive expliciting, you will be able to identity half truth from a whole truth. When I say 'TRUTH'. I mean total truth in this work that is constructively done. Truth is life, arsenal, freedom, joy, happiness and enemy to worry, care, ignorance, anxiety, shadow arsenal and the likes of fear.

1. 'TRUTH' as the saying goes is divided into three types. It contains in its fullness, philosophy, science and religion in perspective. No religion survives without its focus on philosophy and science and it is the same with science as well.

2. A scientist may say he does not believe in God but in the Universal Energy, trying to discrepence science from religion. He may say, he does "not believe in religion at all". Why? Because he thinks that there was an evolution which caused a blast and the earth came into being. At least such scientist should have known that, it was something that caused the so-called evolution.

(Religion, science and philosophy cannot be separated. They are one. The greatest scientist cannot really defined electricity, so is it with religion—that is, the greatest religious leaders cannot really define God. But we must know and understand that every constructive thinker knows that, every effect is from a cause and they all starts with the first cause which is the beginning. Although man does not know where God in religion came from, man must believe he exists. Why? Because man can see the manifestation of God every where around him. With the scientist; even though he cannot really define electricity, he see the manifestation of electricity all around him, even in his house. In this explanation, philosophy can be found and need to be discovered by my precious readers, for philosophy is the love of wisdom. There cannot be a design without a designer or creation without a creator or effect without a cause. Truly, no cause can make the first cause, or the first cause will also become the second cause, which is a mathematical absurdity.)

3. But all the same, in his work, he consciously or unconsciously operates in the modus-operandi of the Universal Law, for one cannot be separated from the other—religion, science and philosophy

4. Again let me say the law, the formula is already been set out already which he just put himself into while working consciously or unconsciously

5. But remember, in this chapter, I mean to clarify it into these: Civil, Moral, and Spiritual. These three fused together is the Universal Truth. Similarly to science, religion, and philosophy fusing together to unfold causes and effects. When one of these is omitted, it is then know as half truth and not the whole truth.

6. As we have been learning from days of old trying to know what we never heard, it was clear and convincing that—Civil truth relates to matters of leadership and justice in countries and kingdoms.

7. Moral truth relates to situation of everyone's life which have regard to companionships and social relations in universal to that which is honest and right, in particular to virtue of every kind.

8. Spiritual truth is related to salvation of heaven and of the church, temple; in general to the good of love and the truth of faith or hope.

9. Great minds in theology, religion and philosophy accept the fact that the law of the good of love and the uses basically means performing one's duty of office to the benefit of

all—trees, water bodies, animals, human beings; the land, the sky and so on.

10. Constructive thinkers know these fact and truth married together from the days of old. They know also that physically the merely natural man lives in accordance with the same commandments in the same way as the spiritual man does, for likeness, he worships the Almighty . . . Allah in religion goes into the temple, the church, the mosque, hears preaching's or teaching, assumes a devout countenance, refrain from committing murder, adultery, theft, from bearing evil witness, from defrauding his neighbours of their goods

11. But let me say this as the truth is, all this he does merely for the sake for himself and the world, to keep up appearance. Inwardly, since in the heart he denies the Universal Law whether consciously or unconsciously, knowingly or unknowing, in worship, he acts the hypocrite, when left to himself and his own thoughts laughs at the holy things of the church, believing that they merely serve as a restraint for the simple multitude.

12. Therefore he is wholly on totally disjoined from heaven thus from the Universal Law; not been observant or a spiritual man he is neither a moral nor civil man.

13. He may refrain from committing murder, he hate everyone who oppose him; from his hatred burns with revenge.

14. He would affect murder had he not been restrained by the civil laws and external bonds which he fears. Like he longs to do so, it follows that he is consistently committing murder. Although he does not affect adultery, yet, like he converts the good of others and not regards fraud and wicked devices as opposed to what is lawful, in intent he is continually acting the thief.

15. This is typically of moral life which forbids false witness and coveting the goods of others. Such is every man who denies the Universal Law; who is got no conscience derived from religion.

16. For this reason, great thinkers came down long ago for the purpose of reducing to order all things in heaven and things in the church, temple and the way of worship. Because in that time, the power of hell prevailed over that of heaven and upon the earth the power of evil over that of good. In consequence of that a total damnation stood threatening at the door. Those impending damnation was why teachers like Jesus Christ, Mohammad and others came through the Universal Law to remove, therefore redeeming angels and men—salvation. But now in this twenty-first (21) century, their teaching is being destroyed by falsification and adulteration of the WORD.

17. Let me tell you another story and it will be your responsibility to identify which is whole and which is not.

18. Long ago, in the land of Iraq there were two great rivers, the Tigris and the Euphrates which join and run into the sea, but in the olden days they entered the sea separately. For a long time this land was called Mesopotamia, which means the Land between the Rivers but today we call it Iraq. From very early times men built great cities along the banks of these rivers. The city had strong wells to keep the enemy out and the house had lovely gardens inside a courtyard. And the people had fine clothes and beautiful jewels to wear.

19. Great Kings ruled over these cities and trained their men to fight as soldiers. The soldiers had spears and shields and fought all together in a square, so that they beat their enemies easily. Thus the Kings conquered other cities and so built up great empires. When they defeated other nations, they often forced the people to come and live in their country and be their servants. And so they had many people to work for them.

20. These people worshiped the sun god, whom they called Marduk. They built high towers, with steps going round them. Therefore the worshippers could climb up high and be nearer the sky. The priests were very learned, and studied the stars. They could count the years, and months and seasons, and make calendars.

21. But they also believed that they could fore-tell the future from the stars, and thought that one star was lucky and another unlucky. One of the greatest of the cities was called Babylon and there lived a famous King named Hammurabi. He was

a great law-giver and made many laws for his people. If one man burnt another, he had to be burnt in turn. If he cut off a man's arm, his own arm was cut off as a punishment.

22. This is the rule called "an eye for eye and a tooth for a tooth". The Babylonians thought that these were wonderful laws, and considered that their god must have help Hammurabi to make them. So they carved a picture showing the god Marduk giving the laws to Hammurabi.

23. Babylon was a great city, and the walls were so wide that five chariots could drive round abreast. One of the later Kings built some beautiful tenaced gardens for his queen. She had felt lonely so far away from her own country, so the King had the gardens made to cheer her up.

24. These gardens became famous all over the world. Another great sight in Babylon was the King's library; but the books were not made of paper, they were all tablets, made of clay baked hard.

25. Long after the days of Hammurabi one of the Kings of Babylon named Nebuchadnezzar fought against the Jews who lived in Palestine, and brought them to live in Babylon. The Jews were so sad at leaving their country that they wrote some beautiful songs of sorrow. One of them begins " By the waters of Babylon we sat down and wept when we remembered Zion"

26. Zion was the name of their own holy city, which is also called Jerusalem. The Jews wrote a record of all that happened. That is how we know so much about Babylon at this time, for these writings have been preserved in that part of the Bible called the Old Testament, Which is the sacred book of the Jews and the Christians.

27. Now remember that civil truths are the civil laws of regions, states, and countries which have relation in brief to many phases of just that one observed, and on the contrary to the various kind of violence that exist in act.

28. Moral truth of a man is of various names known as friendship, diligence, industry, alertness, generosity and so on

29. Spiritual truth is with a man in love of religion, faith, conscience, innocence and many others.

30. It should be known that the basic cause of truth is faith, and faith needs facts to be so for without faith there is no truth. Charity is the foundation upon which faith is built.

    Why? Because faith alone has no place in the order of creation.

31. Charity as experience by great minds in theology consists chiefly in willing well and doing well to the neighbour, in acting in every work from justice and equality, from good and truth, and the like manner in every office—performing uses—prayer

32. An illustration of charity is when a King, president or a judge administers justice for the sake of justice, and if he or she punishes the guilty and absolves the innocent, that is a work of charity; because of this act, he consults the welfare of his follow citizens and of his country—checking of corruption

33. The same applies to the priest, pastor or the imam who teaches truth and leads to good, for the sake of truth and good, performs charity.

34. But he who does the vice versa for the sake of self and the world does not exercise charity, because he does not love his neighbour but himself.

35. This is the same in other things, whether men or women are in any office or not, as with children toward their parents and parent toward their children, with subjects towards their masters and with masters toward their servants, with subjects towards their King and with a King toward his subjects. Whoever of these does his duty from a sense of duty and what is just from a sense of justice exercise charity.

36. A man of business, if he looks to the laws and shuns evil as sins and transacts his business sincerely, justly and faithfully becomes a man of charity—he acts as though from his own authority and yet he trusts in the law.

37. He is neither discouraged in misfortune nor elated with success. He does think of what should be done in morrow,

and how it should be done, yet does not concern himself with morrow because he ascribes the future into the Universal Law, and not to his own power. He loves business as the principle of his talent or vocation and money as its instrument.

38. Charity, which in its importance is the affection of knowledge, understanding, willing and doing truth and good, does not come into any perception of man until it has formed itself in the thought, which is from the understanding. It then present itself under some form or image by which it appears on the mind, for the thought that a thing is so in truth is called faith.

39. Faith is an attitude, a relationship, a confidence or a lifestyle and is more than just excitement, good feeling or hype. Just as prayer is more than talking, because it includes faithfulness.

40. One thing that must be known is that when it comes to the modus operandi of the Universal Law, the laws are just but not fair, even though one may not agree with me now. But if I have a ($10) ten dollar bill, and I want to share it among five people; and I give each person a ($1) one dollar bill, that is fair.

41. But, if I saw the need of one person who needs a ($5) five dollar bill and I give him a ($ 5) five dollar bill, and the others says: "That is not fair," yes it is not fair but I tell you the truth, its just. Why? Because I saw his exact need and I solved or satisfied it. This is one of the greatest modus operandi of the Universal Law.

42. Now in your next exercise, think about your background on how your parent's attitude towards money has influenced or affected your attitude towards money.

43. One of the best ways to plan the future and avoid wasting your hard work is to create a self budget—to put your plans on paper. What fact is stronger than this " real-eye-opener" principle—seeing your income and expenses on paper. This is a scenario:—writing down all your fixed expenses. Agreeing on what percentage of your income should be saved—saving with the bank.

44. Then list your variable expenses, such as food, power or electricity, and phone bill, and then keep track of your actual expenses for a few months. If possible, adjust your lifestyle so that you do not sink into debt.

45. Now learn to open and having an honest conversation about your money with the bank—team work. Consult your bank before making large purchases and think critically of their opinions and feelings. This express trust in each other.

46. Also take into consideration your strengths, and weaknesses, and review the arrangement after a few months. Be surely willing to making any adjustments—sacrifices. In your regular exercises, meditate this way or a better way by developing on this finance and improve on it yourself.

CHAPTER 5

DISCOVER HOW TO ACT IN THE UNIVERSAL LAW TO MASTER YOUR OWN DESTINY

In detail, to obtain the above answer of the problem you cannot escape from the law set for working it out. A good student or learner will follow the law for solving this problem. A good thinker knows that solving this problem begins with the readings from the sleeve which is equal to 7, divided by 2; that is 7/2= 3.5mm. This is the answer because; sleeve reading is always divided by 2. Then to the thimble readings. This reading is equal to 20mm because the dividing line on the sleeve maps or corresponds to 20mm which is always divided by 100 that is $^{20}/_{100}$ = 0.20mm. Now the two results added together gives us the micrometer readings which is equal to 3.7mm—(3.5 + 0.20) mm. This is pure physics practical or practical of wisdom. This is one of the ways of solving life's problems.

(You may develop a new way of doing it but remember that either you used the universally accepted laws as that of the above or not, the above laws cannot be escaped in order to be safe in achieving the correct answer. Well . . . would it not be easier knowing the law and operating in it? It is the truth from wisdom that makes men free forever. If you are ignorant of this law, you will be confused wondering about how to solve such like-manner-problem, when you are confronted with one in life. All the same, the person with the understanding of this wisdom will quickly solve the problem and move on ahead in life leaving you behind. You may cry, complain and so on, but that will not change anything to create any other positive effects. The law is already available to be used. So please go, do your best and know about the law, and use it to your advantage. Humble yourself in silence or before silence to know about or have the law. This is methodical and simple as the Methodist follows the method's of John Wesley to do the wisdom of Jesus Christ. This is like the Muslims following the ways of Muhammad of Islamic region—Their method of worship is universal.)

1. The errors in today's civilization is that, some human individuals tend to feel that with the emergence of civilization and modernity, there should be modifications to the original plan of the Universal Law, concerning the things of the mind which had been made million of years back, they could make some changes that would suit their present tastes and preferences.

2. Can the land on which we walk on today which was from ancient days be changed to become the sky? Can the ancient

sea we know of today be changed into a river or lake?! Right thinkers do not waste time arguing with these ignorant folk; rather, they refer these ignorant back to history, to correct facts and truths with pure standpoints on causes and effects. For instance, the institution of marriage from the ancient days is immutable.

3. Personally, no-body can cajole me from believing like Moses, Jesus, Muhammad did believe in the historicity of Adam and Eve's marriage known in religion which has taken hold of science and philosophy also; which God instituted in 4004 before Christ. Calculates by James Usher, Arc-Bishop of Armah.

4. James Ushers' chronology was added in 1701 to the authorized version of the Bible (1611). This man was a constructive thinker. He worked backwards and reckoned the fact. Can you imagine the genealogies of Jesus Christ in the Bible? Jaram begat Uzziah, where as we know for a fact from the second book of kings that he was actually not his grandfather but his great-great-grandfather. Three complete generations have been left out.

5. It is believed in recent near-eastern studies that such omissions were a regular practice in genealogies and this you must know to understand them for yourself.

6. With this truth, it is clear that any person who changes the correct thoughts in a constructive action of the Universal Law will be unacceptable and will not go unpunished.

7. Shedriach, Meshash, Abednego and Daniel in the Bible's Old Testament days, Mahatma Gandhi, Martin Luther the protestant, Nelson Mandela, Martin Luther King Jr. and Flit. Jerry John Rawlings tried their best to re-correct most of these practices.

8. It is said thousands of years ago and the sayings still holds the same that, "Though they join forces the wicked will not go unpunished; but the posterity of God will be delivered".

9. Wisdom speaks the truth, today; it is more natural for us to think of man as a "Citizen of the World" than in the context of a particular history, especially the history that begins with Abraham.

10. Jesus of Nazareth's quest for wisdom sent him into the wilderness for forty (40) days and forty (40) nights as the story is told and so, philosophers define philosophy as the love of wisdom. Because that is what it literally means. The quest for wisdom is the quest for the meaning of life. It is the basic interest of every human being.

11. Forty (40) days and forty (40) nights? Then, let me tell you a story of a famous scientist who's name is Archimedes who lived many years before the birth of Jesus Christ. He was

one of the great Greek thinkers like Socrates of whom many have heard much of; Archimedes was like Aristotle, a Greek scientist.

12. He lived nearly two hundred years after Greece had begun to lose its importance as a nation. Many Greeks had left their own land and had gone to live in Greek colonies which had been founded in the countries around the shores of the Mediterranean Sea. There the Greek language was spoken and Greek learning was studied. The town where Archimedes was born was one of the biggest and most important of these Greek colonies. It was called Syracuse and was a large and prosperous trading city and seaport in Sicily, an island near the south of Italy.

13. Archimedes' father was an important man in Syracuse. He saw that his son was a very clever boy and he wanted him to have the best education possible, so he sent him overseas to study at the great school of Alexandria in Egypt, one of the cities founded by Alexander the Great when he was on the march with his great army.

14. There he had the good fortune to be under a famous teacher called Conon, who had been a pupil of Euclid, the man who first made Alexandria famous for its mathematical teaching. Archimedes worked hard and made the most of his opportunity and when he returned home to Syracuse, where he spent the rest of his life, he soon became famous himself.

15. The king of Syracuse, whose name was Hiero, was his friend and Archimedes used his knowledge to help the king in all sorts of ways. He had showed that he had great gifts as a mathematician when he was at Alexandria and he carried on his mathematical studies when he got back to Syracuse and soon became the most skilful mathematician living. To please the people of Syracuse he invented many wonderful machines which made them proud of him. The most famous of these machines is a pump known as Archimedes' screw. This was so successful that by turning a handle, a man could pump water that had leaked into ship.

16. The story is told that one day King Hiero asked Archimedes to help him. He had given some gold to a craftsman and asked him to make it into a crown for him. When the craftsman brought back the crown to the palace, King Hiero thought he had mixed some other metal with the gold and had stolen some of the gold for himself. So he asked Archimedes to find out if this had been done.

17. Archimedes could not think how he could find this out and he puzzled and puzzled over it, until one day when he was in the public bath, he saw how the water rose up and flowed over the edges when he stepped into it and that gave him an idea of how he could find out what the king wanted.

18. He was so excited that he got out of the bath and ran home through the streets of Syracuse without his clothes shouting out: "Eureka, eureka" as he ran, which means, 'I have found

it, I have found it'. He took a bowl of water and put the crown in it and measured how much water overflowed from the bowl.

19. Then he filled the bowl up with water again and took an amount of gold equal to the amount King Hiero had given the craftsman and put it in the bowl, by the difference in the amount of water which overflowed from the bowl he found out how much gold had been taken away.

20. When Archimedes was getting to be an old man great trouble came upon Syracuse. At that time war was going on between the Romans who lived in Italy and who were becoming a very strong people, and the people of Carthage in Africa. These Carthaginians were not Africans. They were those whose forefathers had crossed the sea from Asia and settled in North Africa to trade.

21. They were called Phoenicians and their home was in a small country to the north of Palestine. Their chief cities were called, Tyre and Sidon and from these cities their sailors set out on long journeys all over the world. Some of them even came as far as England to buy tin from the people of Cornwall in south-west England from the tin mines there. Others pushed out round the coast of Africa till they reach the Bight of Benin.

22. You can read of them in the Bible, the Book of Kings, where we are told that Hiram, King of Tyre sent cedar wood to King Solomon to help in the building of his temple at Jerusalem.

23. Many of the Phoenicians, like the Greeks, had left home to settle in foreign lands, and just as Syracuse was a Greek city in Sicily, so Carthage was a Phoenician city in Africa. It had become a very rich and powerful place in the time of Archimedes and the Carthaginians and the Romans were fighting to see which of them should be master of the Mediterranean Sea. Carthage had a great general called Hannibal, and he had persuaded the people of Syracuse to make friends with him.

24. The Romans, when they heard this, were very angry with the Syracuse's and they sent ships and soldiers to capture their city. They surrounded Syracuse. Roman ships attacked it from the sea, and Roman soldiers from the land.

25. Archimedes helped the King and his inventions were so clever that it took the Romans three years to capture the city. On one occasion he invented a machine which lifted up the Roman ship right out of the water and dropped them down and sank them.

26. It is also said that he set fire to some of the Roman ships when they came near the city by directing the rays of the sun on to their wooden sides by means of a mirror though this story may not be true.

27. In the end, however, the Romans captured Syracuse because their army was bigger and stronger than the Syracusan army. A man called Marcellus was in command of the Romans and he knew about Archimedes and respected and admired him because of his great learning, and thinking abilities.

28. Before the last attack on Syracuse he gave orders that his soldiers were not to harm Archimedes, but when they went, he was not in his house.

29. He was on the seashore working out a mathematical problem on the sand, and one of the Roman soldiers who did not know who he was killed him with his spear. When Marcellus hear about it he was very sorry and ordered that Archimedes' body should be given honourable burial, and he found his family and helped them.

30. There were many other great scientist who studied at Alexandria in those days. There was Aristarchus who was the first man to discover that the earth moves round the sun and there was Eratosthenes too, who was the first scientist to measure the size of the earth.

31. But Archimedes was the greatest of them all, many of his mathematical engineering discoveries are still in use today.

32. The fundamental interest of every human being brings to mind causes and effects, because, of the Egyptian priest' sign for 'ox' was ◁ and this was altered until it lost two eyes

and was placed on its side ▽. The Hebrew name for this sign was "alif", then, **A**. Therefore the picture of a bullock's head is now the first letter in our alphabet.

33. The histories of other letters can be traced back in the same manner. As it has been said in the above instances, the ancient Egyptian picture-sign for house was a rectangular room with an open doorway [sign]. It was natural for later writers to make this sign more quickly and easily by closing the door and drawing the left side first. This reached Greece under the name 'beta' and so in our letter, b, there are more examples to be talked about. But writings will not permit me to give you the histories of the rest of the alphabets which are very interesting as well.

34. In the oneness of history these alphabets came about to be known for what they stand for today. A musician once said in his music that; 'If you forget your past and histories then you do not know where you are coming from". Yes! It is true, he who forgets his past and histories is like a tree with no or weak root. Such a tree is in danger of any strong or heavy rainfall).

35. **In real wisdom, the way to solve the problems of the world unity is to concentrate on man, whose needs and aspirations are fundamentally or basically the same in all situations and to rule out the memories, loyalties and cultural peculiarities that makes for human diversity and conflict.**

36. The fundamental fact and truth in every religion is to acknowledge God and desist from doing evil to the neighbour. For this reason, the Universal Law makes provisions that, this fundamental fact and truth should be in every religion whether the religion in practice is conscious of Jesus Christ or Mohammed or Krishna consciousness or not.

37. With this wisdom, let me draw you attention back to silence thought. It is the mightiest agent in human affairs truly. This is clearly factual in the case of the wisdom of Job were the devil insinuates that Job's relation to God is not one of unqualified trust 'for better or for worse" but a fail-weather service of God in order to obtain the blessings of health, reputation, family and long life.

38. The nature of Job's faith is explored at much deeper level. Then, after the discussion has ranged through the whole realm of experience God answers out of the whirl wind. (With some people, it could be in a dream or in vision)

39. Job then submits in silence and repents, where upon further meditations or thoughts in the light of the whole composition, which reaches its octave higher, when God speaks and Job humbly repents or return to God. This is theological fact and religiously fatual!

40. Some individuals may say that this was the doings of God. But you should not forget also that the phenomenon is already laid down for every individual to take advantage of it.

41. This is about cause and effect. The law of attraction could not have come into play if Job, had not been operating in that law, he did operate in that law—he did operate in it unconsciously. It would be observed upon further meditation that, Job himself said: 'The things that I feared is come upon me", so you see?!

42. Fear is man's greatest enemy. The devil itself in the mind, and at the bottom of all our worries, cares, in-fact, at the bottom of all negative thoughts or thinking—timidity, cowardice, superstition, anxieties and so on.

43. This was the cause of Job's lost of wealth or back or return to poverty. But after renewing his mind with an all conquering principles of practical and applied physiology, he got back everything that he had lost even several times higher than the already lost ones.

44. The Universal Law is known by what is does or brings to pass. So that, when the question is asked:—What is Universal Law? Would be answered this way—An event that will take place in the future. Let us use religion for an instance here, the name Yahweh is regarded as cult name of the high God, El.

45. It is a cult name because; it is regarded as a holy name and is mentioned of only on serious occasions such as performing the Sabbath worship and the likes. "Adonai" literally meaning "The Lord" replaces the cult name. Even in Christendom,

Adonai (Lord) is still used to replace the cult name—Yahweh / Jahweh with different spellings but the same pronunciation. With the help of a theologian, a philosopher, you will know and understand in discovery of wisdom that, Jehovah is an artificial form that arose from the erroneous combinations of the consonants YHWH with the vowels of Adonai by a Christian during the late thirteenth century after the death of Christ. In English versions, the name is usually recorded as "The Lord".

46. It would be observed in the Bible that when Moses did ask God his name, God never revealed it to him but did reveal his works of wonders before him (Moses). Chase after real power instead of shadow power, or reality instead of fake.

47. Knowing the law does not care about a sinner nor a righteous person. Sinners and righteous people do have dreams, visions and so on. The law have been set into operation. Knowing it and setting yourself to operating in it is all you need. For this reason, in religion, the sinner can be rich as well as the righteous. But the righteous adds to his riches, peace.

48. With a constructive research in the Bible, it is evident that, only in (Ex. 3:13-14) that there is an attempt to explain the name on the basis of the verb "to be, to happen". Name is just an identity for you are not yourself. You are just a material wear to yourself—the physical body shaping the nature of the spiritual.

49. This is mathematically correct to be specific, in Surds. For example;

Identities	Examples
$(\sqrt{a})^2 = a$	$(\sqrt{5})^2 = 5$
$\sqrt{a^2} = a$	$\sqrt{6^2} = 6$
$\sqrt{cd} = \sqrt{c} \times \sqrt{d}$	$\sqrt{9 \times 10} = \sqrt{9} \times \sqrt{10} = \sqrt{3^2} \times \sqrt{10} = 3\sqrt{10}$

50. This means that your life is an example of your identity so that when your name is called to a person, the person simply knows you by your actions whether you are a good or a bad individual—philosophy.

51. Every person operates in his own identity. For this cause you cannot operate in anybody's identity but yours only, for the former can happen only when the environment is ignorant of this truth and laws. You are an individual identity in the Universal Identity as in the examples above.

52. ($\sqrt{a^2} = a$ can also be $(\sqrt{4})^2 = 4$. This is the universality of your identity therefore you must strive with all your arsenal to be yourself in all your actions than someone else's. This makes you unique—making the news for the masses to examine.

53. In life, the quest for success? It is equally important to know what not to do as what to do and this is mathematically exact for example:
$a\sqrt{b} + 3a\sqrt{b} = 4a\sqrt{b}$ but not $8\sqrt{2} + 8\sqrt{3} \neq 16\sqrt{5}$
$6\sqrt{2} + 3\sqrt{2} = 9\sqrt{2}$ but not $\sqrt{4} + \sqrt{6} \neq$
$8\sqrt{3}-2\sqrt{3} = 6\sqrt{3}$ but not $\sqrt{6}-\sqrt{4} \neq \sqrt{2}$,
just because of the statement that Surds are added or subtracted when numbers under root signs are the same.

54. (In mathematics—simplification of algebraic expressions—addition and subtraction—only like terms can be added or subtracted to give a single term and is usually called collecting like terms. In religion, followers of Jesus Christ will gather with Jesus Christ; followers of Muhammad will gather with Muhammad. This is the truth in science—Red and red give more red; green and green give more green and so on.)

55. A Rastafarian will say "I and I" literally meaning he and his spirit or I and my spirit—fusing himself to be one with the spirit in mind. Likewise Jesus of Nazareth—I and my father are one—fusing himself with the spirit to be one form in the mind.

56. A perfect illustration is of man and a woman who have gone through all the laid down procedures of their environment customarily and are therefore recognized as husband and wife, they are no longer two but one—fusion—wisdom.

GOD—The embodiment or some aspect or reality of some being regarded as the ultimate principle of the universe.

Gravitation—Is a natural phenomenon by which all object with mass attract each other, and is one of the fundamental forces of physics.

Arcana—Is a great secret that is hidden from the masses.

Krypton—Is a shining jewel in a dark vast world or universe.

Love—Is the outgoing or the yearning of the heart for that which is good or excellent.

Philosophy—Is the love of wisdom

Religion—Is a continuous process of investigation and experimentation in order to widen people's understanding of the spiritual world.

Science—Is a continues process of investigation and experimentation in order to widen people's understanding of the natural world.

1. Heaven—It is a place or state of bliss.

2. Immutable—It is that which is unchangeable.

3. Solemn—That which is considered to be serious.

4. Reciprocal—It is an agreement binding two parties equally.

5. Faith—It is a trust or believing in something or some aspect.

6. Fact—It is that or something known to be true or correct.

7. Fathom—To understand something or to measure something.

8. Fame—One who is widely known.

9. Neighbor—An individual living near or next to another.

10. Truth—The quality of being true because of true evidence.

11. Meditation—To focus one's mind in silence for relaxation to think deeply.

12. Masses—It is a large group or crowd of people.

13. Miracles—That which is above the natural laws which are attributed to super-natural causes because it beats the imaginations of the natural laws.

14. Hell—It is a place of punishment living wickedly or a state of misery.

15. Chronology—It is the arrangement of events in order of occurrence.

16. Modus operandi—That is a method of working.

17. Consciousness—That is to be in alertness.

18. Unconsciously—When one is not in alert position.

19. Explicit—It is when one speaks plainly.

20. Concentration—That is focusing all of one's attention on a purpose.

21. Spiritual—This is of human spirit or soul.

22. Superstition—This is about believing in magical ideas or practices.

23. Christendom—This involves Christian nations or every Christian.

24. Intellect—It involves the minds power of reasoning.

25. Sin—Is an act of the will in revolt against God.

26. Gods—Is the divine beings in God's heavenly court.

27. Justice—It is the act of being at your rightful place or position.

28. Use—It is to perform one's office and to do one's work rightly, faithfully, sincerely, and justly.

When a thing is ingrained in a person, you cannot convince him against it—Felix Kwesi.

Self interest is an intelligent selfishness—S.K. Tamakloe

Defeat never comes to any man until he admits it—Josephus Daniel

Most of the important things in the world have been accomplished by people who have kept trying when there seemed to be no hope at all—Dale Carnegie

Diligence overcomes difficulties; sloth makes them—Benjamin Franklin

Do not spend the strength of your zeal in censuring others. The man that is most busy in censuring others is always least employed in examining himself—Thomas Lye

The easiest road to hell or suffering is the gradual one—the gentle slope, soft underfoot, without sudden turnings, without milestones, without signposts—C.S. Lewis

No pain, no gain; no thorns, no thrones; no gall, no glory; no cross, no crown—William Penn.

Since our task is difficult, we dare not relax; since our opportunities are brief we dare not delay—Jerry Gavor

No one is living aright unless he so lives that whoever meets him goes away more confident and joyous for the contact—Lillian Whiting

When wealth is lost, nothing is lost, when health is lost, something is lost; when character is lost all is lost—Billy Graham

Let no man imagine that he has no influence whoever he may be, and where ever he may be placed, the man who thinks becomes a light and a person—Amidu Adams

Only those who dare to fail greatly can achieve greatly—Robert Kennedy

When the going gets tough the tough gets going—Robert Schuller

Watch constantly against those things which are thought to be no temptations. The most poisonous serpents are found where the sweetest flowers grow—Charles Spurgeon

When nature is about to do something great, it starts with a difficulty. When it is about to do something truly magnificent, it starts with an impossibility—Amenuku Innocent

Wise people live in wealth and luxury, but stupid people spend their money as fast as they get it—Michael Tamakloe

Gold is tested by fire, and human character is tested in the furnace of humiliation—John Maye

The secret for walking on water is knowing where the stones are—Herb Colien

The religion which fears science dishonours God and commits suicide—Waldo Emerson

The only important method of getting or obtaining effective communication is to rely on feed back—Paul Foe

Material progress with no corresponding moral development is corruption—S.K. Tamakloe

SELECTED BIBLIOGRAPHY

An attempt has been made by the author to mention all important book on Life and History, and most importantly; the list includes selected basic work of appreciation which will be valuable to readers who for the most part is confined to what is available in the UNIVERSAL LAW.

READINGS CHAPTER BY CHAPTER IN NUMBERS

CHAPTER ONE

51. Bernhard W. Anderson (The Living World of the Old Testament—Second Edition). Printed in Hard Cover (hc) in Great Britain by Lowe & Brydone (Printers) Ltd, London, N.W. 10

68-77. MAKERS OF CIVILIZATION. Stories for Reading and Telling Book 2 by M.I. POTTS with Illustrations by VALERIE TAYLOR. Publish by SEDCO Publishing Limited under licence from Longman Group Limited 1976. Pages 107-111

CHAPTER TWO

5. Document from Deeper Christian Life Ministry—Deeper Life Women's mirror.

37-51. MAKERS OF CIVILIZATION—Pages 80-84. Printed in Paper Back (pb).

CHAPTER THREE

15. Basic Religious Teachings of Emanuel Swedenborg (The Essential Swedenborg). Selected and Edited and with an Introduction by SIG SYNNESTVEDT. First and second printing in 1970 and 1977 in United State of America by Twayne Publisher, Inc. and Swedenborg Foundation, Inc. respectively with Cover Designed by Bill Huestis. Pages 62-65

27-50. C.S.S. HIGHAM, Christianity, Landmark of WORLD HISTORY: Pages 61-64; and ISLAM: Pages 73-78. LONGMANS.

CHAPTER FOUR

18-26. C.S.S. HIGHAM, THE RIVER CITIES of IRAQ. Pages 18-22. Made and printed in Great Britain by William Clowes and Sons, Limited, London and Beccles.

CHAPTER FIVE

12-31. M.I. POTTS, ARCHIMEDES, Stories for Reading and Telling (MAKERS OF CIVILIZATION); SEDCO. It is widely told in Ghana High Schools. Pages 52-56

32-33. F.G.F., Oxford English Readers for Africa. Number 3 to 7 of pages 2-6.

ABOUT THE AUTHOR

Born in Agbozume in Ghana, Djabaku Yao Francis is being recognized as a living Ghanaian research personality, who is playing a leading role in his country's political and cultural life since 2008. Perhaps Djabaku Yao Francis has greater insight into or a better right to speak of the Universal Law in our time.

www.ingramcontent.com/pod-product-compliance
Ingram Content Group UK Ltd.
Pitfield, Milton Keynes, MK11 3LW, UK
UKHW040601210726
13854UKWH00008B/1670

9 781477 271179